BEIGHTON

MOULTON ST MARY

REMEMBERED

LIMITED EDITION

Sheila Hutchinson

Front Cover Photograph:
Moulton St Mary Post Office around 1970.

Back Cover Photograph:
Beighton Rectory.

© **Sheila Hutchinson 2015**

ISBN 9780957462335

Published
By
Sheila & Paul Hutchinson
7. Colman Avenue,
Stoke Holy Cross,
Norwich,
Norfolk.
NR14 8NA
e-mail address: sandp@paulsheila.plus.com

Printed
By
Really Useful Print Co. Ltd.
Bessemer Road
Norwich.

ACKNOWLEDGEMENTS

I wish to express my thanks to the following people for supplying information, photographs and contributing to this book, without their help this book would not have been possible.

Sylvia Craske, nee White, Margaret Ward, nee Burton, Peggy Francis, nee Smith, Shirley Crosby, nee White, Pearl Crosby, nee White, Fred Rose, John Pegg, Peter Allard, Desmond Sharman, Eric Wright, Maurice Wright, Dorothy Borrett, Ronnie & Mary Myhill, Jill Baker, nee Borrett, Gordon Carter, Val Mack, nee Shearing, Daphne Carway, nee Smith, Violet Edwards, nee Kemp, Jayne Smith, nee Edwards, Valerie Knights, Ramona Knights, nee Ling, Herbert and Doreen Smith, Corinne Miller, Pam Adlam, John Etheridge, Betty Gathergood, nee James and Ralph James.

REFERENCES AND BIBLIOGRAPHY

Census Returns for 1841, 1851, 1861, 1871, 1881, 1891, 1901 and 1911 at Norfolk Libraries and on the internet.
Various old Norfolk Directories from 1836 to 1937 at the Norfolk Records Office, Norfolk Libraries, and on the internet.
Tithe Maps and Apportionments for Beighton and Moulton St Mary on micro-film at Norfolk Records Office. (MF748-57, MF756-57, MF750-380, MF768-380)
Enclosure Maps for Beighton and Moulton St Mary on the internet at the website www.historic-maps.norfolk.gov.uk
Licence Registers PS8/6/1-4 at Norfolk Records Office.
Other documents at the Norfolk Records Office are identified in the text with NRO prefix.
Websites with useful information include:
www.familysearch.org
www.old-maps.co.uk
www.domesdaymap.co.uk
www.1911census.co.uk

Disclaimer.
The information in this book has been collected from many old documents, maps, websites and people's memories. The author cannot accept responsibility for errors and omissions and apologises for any errors that may be present.
      Every effort has been made to establish copyright for the photographs used in this book. Anyone with a copyright claim is asked to contact the publisher in writing.

INTRODUCTION

The parishes of Beighton and Moulton St Mary were separate until Moulton St Mary was incorporated into Beighton in 1935.

In 2004 the Beighton Parish Council requested a change of name for the parish from 'Beighton' to 'Beighton and Moulton St Mary'. The Broadland District Council consulted the residents for their opinions. 44% of the residents, that replied, opposed the name change compared to only 31% in favour so the district council refused the parish council's request and the parish remains as Beighton.

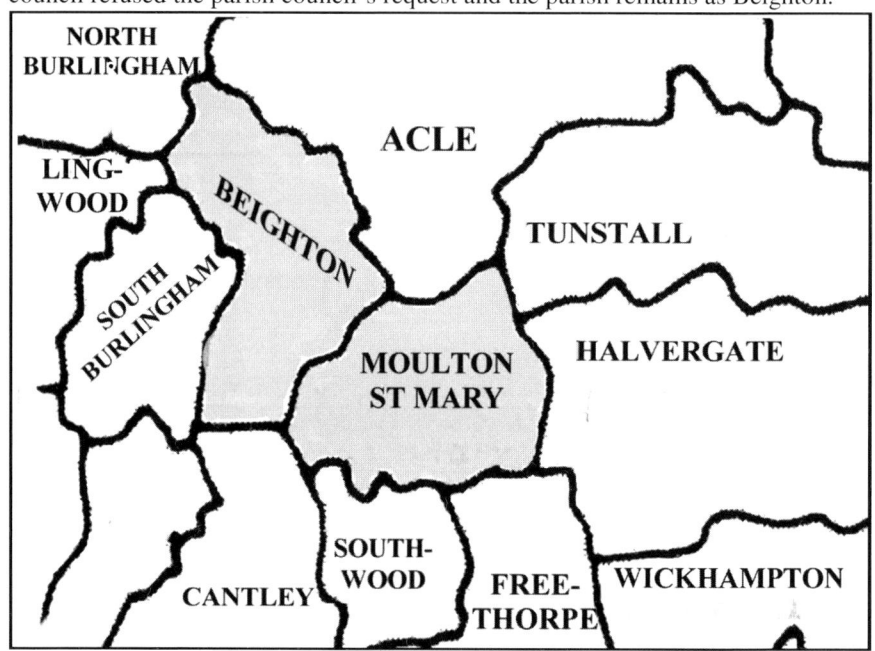

Sketch Map showing the location of Beighton and Moulton St Mary.

BEIGHTON ACREAGE

The area of the old Beighton parish was given as 910 acres in 1831, 1,015 acres in 1851, and 1,029 acres in 1891.

Following the Norfolk County Review of 1935 the area was given as 1,886 acres, after Moulton St Mary was incorporated.

The Beighton Detached marshes, about 94 acres, were lost to Reedham following the Norfolk County Review.

Information from the **Tithe Apportionment** circa 1843:-
Total Area of the parish given as 1015a 3r 3p. Roads and Water occupied 10a 1r 23p. Tithe lands total area 998a 2r 0p comprising 891a 3r 0p Arable, 95a 3r 0p of Meadow, Pasture & Marsh, 2a of Woodland and 9a of Glebe. The crops were

listed as 402.75371 bushels of Wheat, 714.35709 bushels of Barley and 1028.24243 bushels of Oats.

MOULTON ST MARY ACREAGE.

The area of the parish and village from old documents is given as 870 acres in 1831, 1,018 in 1851 and 1039 acres in 1891.
Following the Norfolk County Review Order in 1935, 949 acres of Moulton St Mary was annexed to Beighton and the remote 90 acres of Detached Moulton St Mary marshes were annexed to Reedham parish.
Information from the **Tithe Apportionment** circa 1844:-
Total Area given as 1004a 1r 28p comprising 906a 0r 22p Arable and 98a 1r 6p Meadow & Pasture. The crops were given as: Wheat 349 bushels, Barley 620.378 bushels, and Oats 892.969.

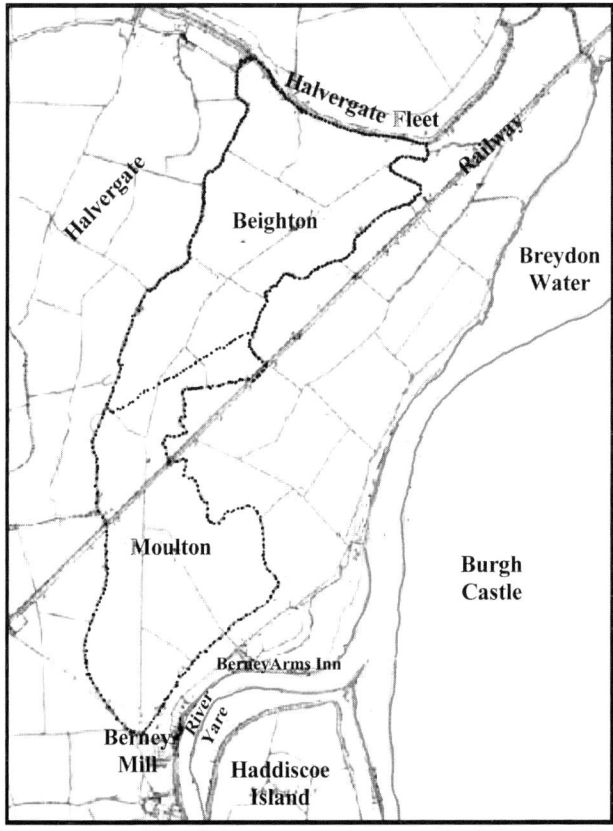

Map showing the location of the detached parts of Beighton and Moulton St Mary. No dwellings existed in these detached parishes.

BEIGHTON

In the Domesday Book Beighton was listed as having 55 households, 29 smallholders, 14 freemen, 2 lord's plough teams, 6 men's plough teams, 16 acres of meadow, and livestock of 16 pigs, 140 sheep and 1 cob.

BEIGHTON RECTORY

The Rectory, located at TG3856508142, was built in 1846 in a Gothic style, constructed with red brick and with a slate roof. It is now a listed Grade II building and a private dwelling called **Cedar House**.

The Beighton Rectory. Supplied by Margaret Ward, nee Burton.

Some occupants after it was sold as a private dwelling include:
Mr Norman Chalk.
Mr & Mrs Arnold in the 1980s.
Mr & Mrs Nash (It was the registered company address for Apex Car Rental Norwich) in 1998.
Cedar House was sold in 1998 for £405,000.

Beighton Clergyman.

Surname	First names	Date	Position	Notes
Gardiner	Germanicus	1582	Rector	
Slynne	Edwardus	1590	Rector	
Slynne	Edwardus	1603	Rector	
Ballard	Simon	1603	Rector	
Reyner	Thomas	1670	Rector	

Beighton & Moulton St Mary Remembered

Surname	First names	Date	Position	Notes
ffeilden	Roberti	1670	Rector	
Essex	Thomas	1675	Rector	
Reyner	Thomas	1675	Rector	
Essex	Thomas	1675	Rector	
Newhowse	Johannes	1681	Rector	
Essex	Thomae	1681	Rector	
Newhouse	Jonathanis	1722	Rector	
Harvey	Calthorpe	1722	Rector	
Burch	Edwardus	1724	Rector	
Rippinghall	John	1733	Rector	
Harvey	Calthorp	1733	Rector	
Gibbon	Thomas	1763	Rector	
Mandeville	Charles	1763	Rector	
Rippingall	John	1769	Rector	
Short	Richard Rider	1769	Rector	
Hurn	William	1781	Curate	
Thurlow	John	1781	Rector	
Goddard	Thomas	1785	Curate	
Short	Richard Rider	1790	Rector	
Buckeridge	Richard	1790	Rector	
Oakes	James	1801	Curate	
Oakes	James	1801	Curate	
Buckeridge	Richard	1803	Rector	
Goddard	Erasmus	1814	Curate	
Buckeridge	Richard	1822	Curate	
Buckeridge	Richard	1824	Rector	
Fellowes	John	1824	Rector	
Goddard	Erasmus	1825	Curate	
Goddard	Erasmus	1827	Curate	
Fellowes	John	1827	Rector	
Buckle	Thomas Starling	1827	Rector	
Fellowes	Thomas Lyon	1845 & 1864	Rector	Residing at Lingwood till 1845. Age 43 in 1861.
Gillett	Edward	1845	Curate	
Burroughs	Robert	1871 & 1877	Rector	age 34 in 1871
Fellowes	Henry Cecil	1879	Rector	
Fellowes	Alfred Lyon	1886	Rector	Age 30 in 1891.

7

Beighton & Moulton St Mary Remembered

Surname	First names	Date	Position	Notes
Nevill	Ralph William	1899 & 1925	Rector	Age 49 in 1911.
Walker	William Robert	1930s		
Greenland	Martin	2010s		

Cedar House, formally the Beighton Rectory.

ALL SAINTS CHURCH BEIGHTON

The Parish church is located at about TG38660829 on Church Hill.
This is a 14th century building of flint with limestone dressing with much later modifications and repairs. It consists of a west tower, porch, aisles, nave and chancel. The nave roof is thatched with eyebrows over the clerestory windows and is supported by 28 original 14th century single-framed scissor braced collar rafters. The rest of the roof is slates.
    Some restoration was undertaken in 1847 at a cost of £2000.
Rebuilding of the north aisle and the part of the tower was carried out in about 1881 by architect A. S. Hewitt.

Beighton & Moulton St Mary Remembered

Postcard views of All Saints Church.

Planting a copper beech tree on the Church Triangle in 1999 to commemorate Princess Diana. The money £25 was provided by Broadland Council. From the left: Donald Borrett, Ronnie Myhill, Bertie Key, Mary Myhill, and David 'Bubbles' Hanton. Photograph supplied by Val Mack.

The square tower, which contains one 6 cwt bell dated 1625, was raised in 1890 and the pinnacles surmounted by stone figures. There is a 13th century font with later oak cover. A Bishop's Cross is painted on the South wall. The Victorian pews in the nave and aisles have a great variety of poppy-head ends. In the North-west corner are two finely carved pew ends, one depicting a sow feeding 10 piglets and the other a dog. The Screen was restored in Victorian times with a crucifixion scene on top with four attendant figures. In the Chancel there is Victorian carving with six stained glass windows showing the Apostles and a fine stained-glass East window.

SOME EARLY BEIGHTON CHURCHWARDENS

Name	Date	Name	Date
Samuel Fowler	1730s	Robert Nudd	1760s
John Ellis	1760s	J. Stratford	1770s
William Fowler	1770s	Robert Ellis	1790s
Robert Howard	1800s		

BEIGHTON SCHOOL, TG 3849 0824

The Beighton School was built in 1856 by the Rev. Thomas Lyon Fellowes. It was a National School. The Plaque on the school records the construction as AD 1856. The school was conveyed to the minister and the churchwardens from Robert Howard on the 29th September 1856. It cost £200 to build and was to accommodate up to 76 children. It was a redbrick, slate and tiled, single storey building with one classroom but with a small lending library above the entrance porch. There is a bell tower over the gable end and main entrance to the building. Plans, elevations and sections of the building are shown in the 1856 document NRO/ P/BG/8. This shows that the building had separate entrances, yards and toilets for boys and girls; a large fireplace in the centre of the classroom and a coalbunker by the girls entrance. The plan indicates that the classroom could, or should, have a raised section in the centre for the infants and have curtains to separate the room into three areas, each about nine feet wide.

The Old School after conversion to a dwelling.

In 1902 Mr Arthur Shearing was appointed by the education committee as County Manager for the Beighton School.

In 1903 the school was in need of repairs; and again in 1926 the Education Committee commented that the building was unsound with cracks in the walls and a leaking roof and was in urgent need of repairs.

The school cleaner in 1918 was a Mrs Elizabeth Griffin. She was paid at 19s 6d per month, but if the building was used for other meetings outside school hours she was to be paid extra according to the extra work required.

Mrs P. Hollis was appointed as the school cleaner in 1926.

In 1927 the Education committee proposed that the infants should use the nearby Parish Room to relieve overcrowding in the school.

By 1947 the school had become redundant, and on 22nd March 1949 the disused school was put up for sale by auction at the Royal Hotel in Norwich.

Mr Harry Buxton purchased the property for £520. After the sale expenses were taken the proceeds of the sale £453 9s 8d were put into a trust called the 'Beighton Old National School Foundation', and this was invested into 2.5% defence bonds.

The old school house was converted into a three bedroom domestic dwelling.

**Miss Cripsey and her class at Beighton School:
Raymond Brown, Leslie Hubbard, Shirley White, Peter James, Peggy Jermy, Keith Dye, and David Hanton.**

Mr Hollis was a recent occupant of the dwelling, and Mr & Mrs Marcus Boddy occupied the old school house from about 2000 and ran a management consultancy business called 'We Manage Quality Limited' from the premises till about 2012.

The property was sold in January 2012 for £270,000.

SOME BEIGHTON SCHOOLTEACHERS INCLUDE:

Name	Dates listed	Comment
Elizabeth Pipe	1858- 1871	Age 34 in 1871, Mistress.
L. P. Gedge	1877	Mistress.
Charlotte Milne	1879 - 1881	Mistress
Susan Whitworth	1883	Mistress
Ellen Hume	1890- 1891	Age 27 in 1891 mistress.
Emma Browne	1891	Age 21, teacher.
Mary J. Hume	1891	Pupil teacher, age 14
Margaret Watson	1896	Mistress
Lorna E. Buck	1900 –1901	Age 48 in 1901.
Alice Read	1901	Age 16, school teacher.
Clara Myhill	1901	Age 14, teacher.
Ada M. Myhill	1901	Age 16, teacher.
Emily Claxton	1904	Mistress.
Miss Lucy Buckle – Mrs Lucy Chapman	1907- 1930s	She came as a teacher in 1907 directly from Norwich Training School. She was aged 25 in 1911. She married Herbert Chapman in 1911.
Mrs Maud Gilbert	1922 to 1930s	Appointed Assistant teacher in October 1922 at £90 per annum. Infant teacher. Also at Moulton.
Mrs Ruby Ling	1940s	Also teacher at Moulton
Miss Muriel G Hargrave	1936	Appointed as Head Mistress in January 1936.
Miss Lettall	c.1940	Head teacher.
Miss Enid M. Stokes	1942	Appointed as Assistant teacher In December 1942.
Miss Cripsey	1940s	
Miss Thirza Bond	1940s	Head teacher.

Beighton School photograph believed to be from the 1920s.
Photograph supplied by Val Mack.

Left: Beighton School Headmistress Mrs Lucy Chapman, formerly Miss Lucy Buckle. Photograph from Pearl Crosby, nee White.

Beighton School photograph supplied by Ronnie Myhill. Standing from the left: Dennis Futter, Dorothy Dye, John Stone, Ronnie Myhill, Rita Hubbard, Freda Lane, Geoffrey Stone, Fay Brown, Jean Osborne, Betty Futter. Seated: ? Osborne, Harold Hanton, Frank Osborne, Jimmy Hubbard, Keith Dye, Ray Brown, David Hanton, Pearl White, Peggy Jermy, Betty Jones. Below: Beighton Sunday School Outing. Supplied by Ronnie Myhill.

BEIGHTON METHODIST CHAPEL

Beighton Chapel. Photograph supplied by Margaret Ward, nee Burton.
This was located at about TG383074 on the road now known as Chapel Road. It was built in 1862 of red brick with a slate roof and at a cost of £200. Above the door is a plaque: 'Primitive Methodist Chapel 1862'. This was built on area 158 on the Tithe Map, which had a cottage occupied by the Gilbert and Eccleston families and was owned by Robert Howard at that time. In the altered Tithe of 1886 this plot was owned by Mary Magdalene College and occupied by Samuel Wright.

It was attached to the Yarmouth Circuit till 1883 when it became under the Acle Circuit. A school room was included and was used as a Sunday school. The Sunday school was abandoned in 1966 and services were halted in 2005. There was a harmonium made by Estey Organ Co. of Vermont in the USA.

The disused chapel was sold and converted into a private dwelling.
Mr Andy Pearce was the occupant of the Old Chapel in 2008.

Awaiting the last service at the Beighton Chapel which took place on 13th March 2005. Photograph supplied by Val Mack.

WHITE HOUSE (BEIGHTON HOUSE)

This is located at about TG377099, adjacent to the junction of B1140 and the A47.
 This was referred to on the old OS maps as **Beighton House** and was in later years renamed as the **White House**.
 No buildings were here when the Enclosure map was drawn up in about 1801 and no buildings were shown on Bryants Map of 1827. The field here was owned by a Mr Thomas Miles at the time of the Enclosure.

Buildings, however, were shown here on the Beighton Tithe Map of circa 1843 on the area marked as no. 2 area which was then owned by Edmund Miles and occupied by William Miles and was listed as the **Nelson Inn**.

According to the 1835 and 1852 electoral registers an Edmund Miles, a retired royal navy officer living in Blofield, was listed as having a freehold house and land in Beighton near the Norwich Turnpike Road, so the buildings here must have been erected sometime in the early 1830s.

In the 1853 and 1855 electoral registers this Edmund Miles was, however, listed as having moved into this dwelling at Beighton.

Prior to this time a William Miles was listed as an innkeeper or publican in the 1841 and 1851 census returns at Beighton and he is believed to be the occupant here, presumably till Edmund Miles moved here in 1853. This was the **Lord Nelson Tavern** at that time.

Some later occupants include:
Mrs Martha Suffield Miles, the widow of Edmund Miles. She was listed living here in the 1861 census and until her death in 1893, age 84. In 1865 a Mrs Miles was listed as a shopkeeper so the property may have been used as a **shop** for a brief time after the property stopped being a public house. In the 1881 census returns she is in fact listed as a retired publican's widow, suggesting her late husband Edmund was the publican here for a short time.

Her niece Miss Anna Catherine Roberson also lived here with Mrs Miles, and she continued to live here after her aunt's death. She was still listed here in the 1925 directory. Miss Roberson employed Ethel Weavers as her cook. On one occasion Miss Roberson was attacked by someone so she had extra locks fitted on all the doors.

Lacey M. Vincent was listed as the occupant of Beighton House in the 1933 and 1937 directories. His brother was at one time the Mayor of London.

The White House was put up for sale by auction at the Royal Hotel in Norwich in July 1951 Ref. NRO/MC39/175,478X3. The property at that time was described *as Brick and slate construction with six bedrooms, a hall, lounge, dining room, morning room, kitchen, store room, cellar with a WC and bathroom. Water was from a well and pumped into tanks in the roof space. Outside a courtyard, a shed and several outbuildings including a stable, garage, coal house, wash house Fowls house and an earth closet. Large Garden, Orchard and arable land.*

Drainage was via a cesspit and there was a petrol driven electricity generation plant which provided 50 volt dc. The total area was 2 acres and 2 rod.
The Knights family have been here for many years.
The old Coach House at the White House was converted into a dwelling in the late 1990s.

VALERIE KNIGHTS REMEMBERS

We came from Yarmouth in June 1940 after an officer in the army, who was a family member, told us that we must move as the Germans were expected across the North Sea any minute. My step-father was a dentist in Yarmouth and sadly in October that year he was killed in a car accident on his way home. He had suffered a heart attack while driving and was only in his forties.
Early in the war a bomb was dropped half in the field and half in the road next to our property making a very large hole. During the Sunday afternoon following a great many people came to see the damage, Fortunately a farmer living at Cox Hill farm, who was an air raid warden walked across the field towards our house, Beighton House, and noticed a hole which he thought contained an unexploded bomb: he immediately cleared the area of people, and within minutes the bomb exploded so many lives were saved.
Beighton House was once a coaching inn called the Lord Nelson as there was ample stabling. The licence was later transferred to another property in Beighton which was locally known as the "Cold Blow". It was in the 1920s run by a family of the name of Waterson. The man worked on a farm at Upton for a man by the name of Hewitt. Mr Waterson looked after a stallion, and I can remember as a girl seeing him in a pony and trap leading this enormous horse on a line. One day he set off to visit farms in the Freethorpe area and sadly had a stroke. The pony, however, brought him home with the stallion much to the surprise of his wife. Unfortunately nobody could be found to look after the stallion and it had to be put down.
The sugar beet factory at Cantley was a tremendous asset to the local families. It helped with crop rotation and was more profitable than corn. It was labour intensive, but provided work for local people, both in chopping out in the spring and pulling and topping in winter, together with shift work at the factory.
Just after the First World War there were many horses which were injured on the battlefields which needed much care. It was decided to allow the army to provide a hospital for sick horses at Beighton House as there was ample stabling and a pasture.
In the meadow at Beighton House, I asked a man with a digger to pull out a driveway for a house we were building. When I took him a drink he asked me if I had buried an animal. I said, "What a cat or a dog?" "No", he said, "A large animal with great big bones!" So a horse must have died and was buried in the meadow.

The Burlingham village blacksmith gave us a photograph of the horses standing in the courtyard along with the soldiers.

One day during WWII I was alone, about 15 years old, when a man about in his thirties came to the door and asked for something to eat. I made him a sandwich and he sat on an old chair near the backdoor. It was a hot day and I thought, "Why wasn't he in the army?" We were quite used to old tramps coming past on their way to the Lingwood Workhouse. My parents had gone to the village on bikes, so I went to find them as I thought this man was suspicious. So they biked to Acle overtaking the man and spoke to a police officer who they knew. He decided to apprehend the man and the PC brought him to Acle Police Station. He had a knapsack so they asked him to unload it. They were surprised to find pies, sandwiches and a Mills bomb complete with the pin in (grenade)! When asked about it he said if anyone refused to give him something to eat he would threaten them!

In about 1920 Norfolk County Council decided to buy two large estates which came up for auction at the same time. These were the Burroughes family Burlingham Hall Estate and the Jary Estate in the next villages: a total of about 5000 acres. This meant that fields were divided to give a small acreage up to 50 acres for soldiers who came out of the war. Many of the large houses were also divided up.

In WWI the property at Beighton House was used as a hospital for injured war horses. Photograph supplied by Valerie Knights.

BEIGHTON SHOPKEEPERS

There have been a number of shops in the village over the years.
In the 1881 census returns four properties were listed as shops but the locations were not specified.
Today the village has no shops.

Some Shopkeepers from old documents include:

Name	Dates listed	Notes
James Howard	1836 1868	& farmer. Lived at Worlds End. But location of shop not given
Elizabeth Curtis *	1851	Age 40, grocer.
Mrs Miles	1865	At the White House
John Myhill	1865 1896	Age 63 in 1891. & Hay Dealer. & Road Surveyor in 1890.
Robert Read	1861 1890	Age 46 in 1861, & beer retailer at the Nelson public house.
James Youngs	1861 1900	Age 60 in 1891, & farmer.
Elizabeth Carter	1871	Age 59.
William Howard Spooner	1877 1881	Age 29 in 1881, grocer.
Benjamin Curtis	1890	
Elizabeth Curtis *	1891	Age 81, widow of Benjamin.
Mathew Hovells	1896 1904	& publican at the Nelson.
Mary Myhill	1901	Age 73. High Road.
Mrs Mary Ann Youngs	1904	Widow of James.
Robert Read	1904 1908	& publican at the Nelson.
Arthur Shearing	1908 1916	Age 29 in 1911. Chapel Road.
Robert Myhill	1911	Age 50, at Cantley Corner.
Edward Cator	1922 1940s	Near the Chapel.
Herbert Futter	1940s	& post office. Near the Chapel.

Beighton & Moulton St Mary Remembered

Top : Cator's Shop. Supplied by Margaret Ward, nee Burton.

Bottom : Herbert Futter in front of the Beighton Post Office. Photograph from Dorothy Borrett.

BEIGHTON POST OFFICE

No post office was marked on the circa1885 OS map but a letter box was marked close to Stone Corner.

The 1900 directory states: *"James Hubbard, sub postmaster – Letters through Norwich, via Acle, arrive at 7:45 am; dispatched 3:30pm. No Sunday dispatch. Postal Orders are issued here, but not paid. The nearest money order and telegraph office is at Acle"*

The early post office was located on Church Hill as one of the row of terraced cottages and is shown on the 1907 OS map. The post office was probably at this location when the circa 1885 OS map was drawn since James Hubbard who was the sub postmaster in 1883 lived in this row of cottages.

The Post Office was later located on Chapel Road.
From 1957 the Post Office was at the closed Nelson public house building.

Some Beighton postmasters include:

Name	Date listed	Notes
William Barker	1854 -1858	& tailor.
Mrs Maria Neave	1861 - 1868	Age 42 in 1861, deputy postmistress.
	1871	No postmaster listed in census!
	1881	No postmaster listed in census!
James Hubbard	1883 –1904	Age 54 in 1891, sub postmaster & gardener. (He was listed as unemployed in 1881!)
Miss Alice Howe	1908	Sub postmistress.
Miss Florence Sharman	1911- 1912	Age 47 in 1911.
Mrs Priscilla Myhill	1916	Sub postmistress.
Walter Wymer	1922- 1925	Sub postmaster.
Mr & Mrs Herbert Futter	1940s	Chapel Road post office.
Leslie Carway	1957	Located at the old pub.

Dorothy, 'Betty', Borrett, nee Futter worked at the post office and delivered telegrams during the War years. Ted Futter delivered the post around Beighton and Moulton in the 1940s. Leonard Futter also delivered the post when his father retired.

There is no longer a post office in the village and today the post is delivered from Acle.

Ted Futter's retirement from the Beighton Post Office. From the left: Dorothy 'Betty' Borrett carrying Jill Borrett, Mervyn Borrett, Andrew Futter being carried by Shirley Futter, Ted Futter, Mr Shearing and Lenny Futter. Photograph supplied by Jill Baker, nee Borrett.

Mrs Emma Futter, nee Langham, at the old Beighton post office in May 1977. Photograph supplied by Jill Baker.

Beighton & Moulton St Mary Remembered

Top: Lenny Carter, Gorden Beck, Robbie Fransham & Don Borrett.
Bottom: Dennis Grint, Dorothy Dye, Don Borrett & Betty Borrett.
Photographs supplied by Jill Baker.

25

LORD NELSON

Beighton had a public house known variously as the **Nelson**, the **Nelson Tavern** and the **Lord Nelson**.

The first public house was originally at the location of the White House near the A47 road and is believed to have first opened as a public house in about 1838 supplied by brewers Steward & Patteson.

From about 1853 the public house was relocated at a building at about TG379072 and which was listed in the voters register of 1854 as occupied by Robert Read the copyholder of a 'public house and land on Southwood Road'. This building was not in existence at the time when the Tithe map was drawn. It was built on area 179 of the tithe map.

The owners of this property are recorded as Robert Read, then Elizabeth Hovells, a daughter of Robert Read, and then Lacons Brewery.
The pub was often referred to as the **'COLD BLOW'**.

When the pub closed Lesley Carway bought the building from Lacons brewery and it became a shop and post office.

Today it is a private dwelling known as **Nelson House**. The current occupant is Mr Mike Spinks.

Licensee / Publican	Dates Listed	Notes
William Miles	1841 1851	Age 52 in 1851. (Now the White House)
Edmund Miles	1853	Now the White House.
Robert Read	1854 1890	& grocer, age 46 in 1861.
Mathew Hovells	1 Sept 1890	Age 34 in 1891 & shopkeeper. His wife was Elizabeth, daughter of Robert Read.
Robert Read	7 Nov 1904	
Timothy Charles London	17 May 1909	Age 56 in 1911.
Arthur George Waterson	7 Nov 1927	
George Pitcher	15 Nov 1943	
Albert Robert Nickerson	3 Jan 1949	
Stanley Charles Quantrill	1 Jan 1951	
Henry Atkins	14 Jan 1952	
H. Burgess	9 March 1953	
Lesley Howes Carway	7 April 1953	
	1 Mar 1955	Closed by Lacons Brewery. Later converted into a shop & PO.

BLACKSMITHS & WHEELWRIGHTS

The Beighton blacksmith's shop was located at the junction of Southwood Road with High Road at about TG379072.

No building was shown at this location on the Enclosure Map of circa 1801, but it was shown on the Tithe Map of circa 1843 at area 185, owned by Cyrus Gillett and occupied by Brundell and Goff. The blacksmith's shop and house must have been built here sometime after 1801 and before 1843.

The buildings at this location are now called the 'White House' and it is a private dwelling.

Some Beighton blacksmiths include:

NAME	DATES LISTED	COMMENTS
Benjamin Blake	1814 1819	Blacksmith
Roger Smith	1816	Blacksmith
James Myhill	1816 1818	Blacksmith
John Rushmer	1823	Blacksmith
Robert Brundell	1836 1854	Blacksmith (& wheelwright in 1854)
Alfred Tipple	1831 1836	Wheelwright
James Goff	1831 1854	Wheelwright
George Robert Brundell	1858 1864	Blacksmith & wheelwright. Age 21 in 1861, employs 7 men & 1 boy.
Charles Tills	1861	Blacksmith, age 20.
William Lansdell	1861	Blacksmith, age 32.

NAME	DATES LISTED	COMMENTS
Mathew Barker	1861 1901	Wheelwright, age 26 in 1861. Later as Blacksmith, wheelwright & carpenter.
Ellis Peacock	1850 1871	Wheelwright, age 41 in 1861.
Mrs Mary Ann Brundell	1864	Widow of George Robert Brundell. She ran the business.
Daniel Peacock	1866 1879	Blacksmith & Wheelwright, age 46 in 1871
Obediah Peacock	1871	Wheelwright, age 16.
William Bully	1871	Age 48, Blacksmith.
Robert Barker	1881	Wheelwright & carpenter, age 42.
Walter Peacock	1881 1883	Blacksmith, age 23 in 1881.
Alfred Stevens	1881	Age 25, Blacksmith.
Harry Jones	1894	Wheelwright
Robert Tills	1904	Blacksmith
Alfred Youngs	1908	Blacksmith
Albert Welton	1911	Age 34, Blacksmith.
Albert Key	1912	Blacksmith, (age 22 in 1911 carpenter.)
Herbert Chapman	1916 1922	Wheelwright, carpenter, builder & undertaker.

BEIGHTON FARMERS

Many of the occupants were listed in the census returns, directories and other records as farmers. Some only farmed a few acres and some a few hundred acres. In the table that follows the names are given along with known dates and where possible the location is given in the notes.

NAMES	DATES LISTED	NOTES
Samuel Howard	1813 1828	
William Fowler	1815 1871	Age 67 in 1851 farmed 65acres
Samuel Fowler	1827	Stones Corner.
James Enoch Littlewood	1828 1833	Manor House.
Benjamin Heath Baker	1825 1828	
Thomas Archer Walker	1835	Walkers Farm, now Grange Farm

NAMES	DATES LISTED	NOTES
William Stratford	1807 1841	Age 80 in 1841, Lincoln Hall.
William Read	1841	Age 60
James Howard	1841 1869	Age 64 in 1851, 30 acres
Samuel Hewitt	1836 1841	Age 75 in 1841
John Willgress	1841 1850	Age 35 in 1841, Stones Corner
John Slipper (or Skipper?)	1835 1846	Age 25 in 1841, Manor House £50 occupier
Mrs Mary Walker	1841 1845	Walkers Farm, (Grange Farm).
Robert Howard	1845	
Herbert Dixon	1850	
William Dan Fowler	1858 1879	Stones Corner.
James Howard	1854 1868	
Samuel Fowler	1851	Age 22 77acres
James Carver	1824 1854	Age 61 in 1851, 34acres
William Read	1851 1854	Age 70 in 1851, 10acres
Edmund Miles	1854	
John Warnes	1846 1867	Age 41 in 1851, 90 acres.
George Warnes	1863	
Henry Wright	1865	
Thomas Gillett	1864 1883	Near the Church
Hubert Cyrus Howard Gillett	1879 1890	Near the Church
Robert Capon	1868 1883	£50 occupier.
Henry William Ward	1877	
Mrs Capon	1883	
Robert Wright	1879	
Ephraim Lake	1880 1915	Low Farm. Then later at 'Fowlers Farm' age 72 in 1911
John Read	1883 1900	
Richard Wright	1883 1893	
James Youngs	1871 1900	Farmer & grocer.
Albert G. Chapman	1891 1896	Age 27 in 1891.
William Hayden Cooper	1900 1916	Coxhill Farm, age 39 in 1911.
Samuel R. Wright	1898 1916	'Church Farm' age 43 in 1911.
Fullard John Porter	1896 1902	Age 56 in 1901, Near Church.
Henry Edrich	1896	
Gerrard T. Blake	1896 1900	
John Myhill	1901	Age 75.
Mrs Ellen Harrison	1901 1914	Age 58 in 1911, 'Blakes Farm'.
Edward Chaplin	1904	

NAMES	DATES LISTED	NOTES
Henry Sanderson	1904 1916	'Manor House' age 50 in 1911
John Wright	1904 1916	& builder, age 61 in 1911
William Loades	1911	Age 45, at Worlds End
Albert Key	1916 1925	
William Youngs	1916 1922	Church Farm
Herbert Daniels	1916	
Walter Youngs	1922 1937	Coxhill Farm
Arthur Shearing	1922 1940s	Manor House
Edward Wright	1922 1933	Low Farm. Born 1861, a son of Samuel & Sarah Wright.
Arthur L. Shearing	1950s	Manor House
EARP Co. Ltd.	1937	Low Farm
Paul & Val Mack		Manor House

LOW FARM

The original farmhouse was located at about TG383085 on the east side of the B1140 road, Coxhill Road.
    At the time of the Enclosure map it was owned by John Green.
On the tithe map the farmhouse was shown on area 62 and was shown as owned and occupied by Cyrus Gillett. Cottages were shown on the nearby areas 60 and 66 and these were part of the farm property owned by Cyrus Gillett.
Ephraim Lake is believed to have farmed here for a while and then Mrs Ellen Harrison was at the farm as a tenant to Mr Gerrard F. Blake. Mr Blake lived at Bramerton Hall.

    When the farm was put up for sale in 1936 it was described as:
'Farmhouse comprising 3 reception rooms, 5 bedrooms, kitchen, Dairy, Scullery with pump, pantry, storeroom, cellar, lavatory and bathroom with courtyard, out houses, thatched riding stables, 2 boxes, garage, harness room, 3 bullock yards, turnip house, cow house, piggeries, chaff house and wagon and cartlodge.
The farm included a brick and thatched double cottage occupied by Mr Hubbard and Mr Weavers, and a brick and tiled double cottage occupied by Mr Futter and Mr Able. The farm property was in total 176a 0r 18p.'
    The East Anglian Real Property Co. Ltd. bought the farm from Frances Anna Wright, the widow of farmer Edward Wright, the property being conveyed on 13th October 1936 to EARP Co Ltd.
    The EARP Co. Ltd. soon demolished the old farmhouse and the thatched cottages. A large Dutch Barn was erected where the house had stood.

In May of 1978 the remaining farm dwelling on the west side of the road was put up for sale by auction by EARP Co. Ltd. along with 1.662 acres of land. The property had been converted from a double dwelling into a single house and was again called Low Farm.

Large barn where Low Farm existed.

The property had been modernised in about 1966 and was now a 4 bedroom house with mains water, electricity, oil-fired central heating, a telephone and drainage into a septic tank. It included a paddock and a garage.

Mr George Weavers was the occupant in the 1940s.

Duncan Mallett and Josephine Keel of Horsey had an interest in the property in 2004. The property was up for sale in 2005 for £405,000 and again in 2011 for £485,000.

A recent occupant of the property was Mr Timewell.

A recent photograph of Low Farm.

CHURCH FARMS

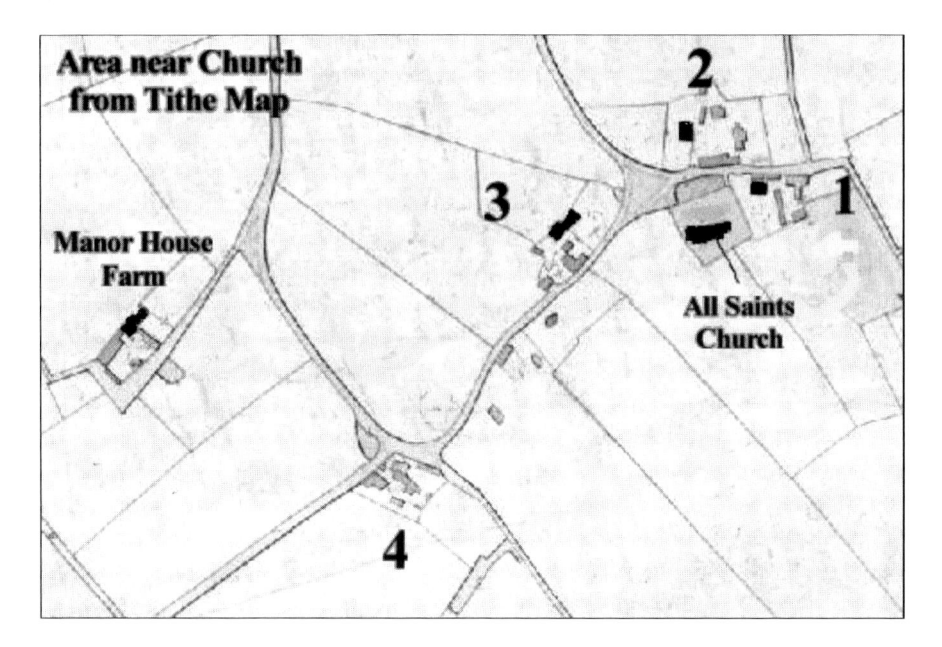

[Map showing area near Church from Tithe Map, with Manor House Farm, All Saints Church, and locations numbered 1 to 4]

Near the church there were 4 farmhouses originally. These are marked on the copy of the Tithe map shown here as numbered 1 to 4.

The first of these, **1** on the above map, was located to the east of the church and was shown on the Enclosure Map as owned by Richard Fowler. He died in 1817 and left his estate to his son William.

On the Tithe map it was listed on area 88 as 'Farmhouse' owned and occupied by William Fowler, a son of Richard and Susan Fowler. William, born in about 1784, was still listed here in the 1861 and 1871 census returns as a retired farmer. William Daniel Fowler, a son of William, was a later owner and is listed as the owner of the farm in the 1874 and 1884 voter's registers.

The early OS maps suggest that this was called Church Farm.

The farmhouse and other farm buildings that were here have been demolished.

The second farmhouse, **2,** was located to the north of the church at about TG387084.

On the Enclosure map it was shown as belonging to Robert Howard jnr. Located on the Tithe map at area 86 and marked as 'House and Premises', it was shown as the property of Cyrus Gillett, a son-in-law of Robert Howard.

On the voters registers of 1861 to 1876 was listed a Thomas Gillett of Trowse as a £50 Occupier: he was one of Cyrus Gillett's sons. He was later listed as the owner.

Hubert Cyrus Gillett, a grandson of Cyrus Gillett was listed as the £50 occupier of the property from 1878 till 1889. This property was shown on the more recent maps as '**Church Farm**'.

Samuel Robert Wright born in 1867 at Beighton, a son of Samuel and Mary Ann Wright, but living in Moulton, had the property at the turn of the twentieth century.

Mr H. M. Wright was the occupant in the 1940s.
The Wright family held the property for many years but a Mr Cator became the occupant around the late 1990s.

The third farm property, **3**, was located to the west of the church. This was shown on the Enclosure map as the property of Robert Howard Snr. On the tithe map the buildings were shown on area 81 as 'Farm Yard and Premises' owned by Robert Howard. This became a row of five cottages at this location sometime before the 1880s OS map was drawn.

The first Beighton post office was located in one of these cottages for many years. This row of cottages has since been demolished.

House at Stone Corner. supplied by Margaret Ward, nee Burton.

The fourth farm, **4**, some distance to the southwest of the church was at about TG384081, at the crossroads often referred to as **Stone or Stones Corner.**

This was at the time of the Enclosure the property of William Fowler of Great Yarmouth. William was a brother of Richard Fowler above. Following William's death the property passed to his nephew Samuel Fowler, a son of Richard Fowler. On the Tithe map and Apportionment the property was listed on area 116 as owned by the executors of Samuel Fowler and occupied by John Willgress. John Willgress married Samuel's widow Mary in 1838. Samuel and

Mary's son, William Fowler, was later the farmer here. He was listed in the 1861 census, aged 29. This farm was sometimes called Fowlers Farm.

The dwelling at Stone Corner has long been semi-detached cottages.

Another view of Stone Corner, supplied by Dorothy Borrett.

MEMORIES BY RALPH JAMES

Ralph James lived at Stone Corner. He milked the cows on the farm, prepared and cooled the milk and then took it to Bessie and Bertha Shearing (mother and daughter) who bottled it at the kitchen table before he then delivered it on his bike, which had a large basket on the front, to many households in the village of Beighton. He can remember to this day names of all those to whom he delivered milk.

He used to go to Mr. Cator at the stores, for his mother, to buy a quarter of gun powder to light the oven; they shut the door quickly as there was a bit of a bang! As a child he saved the house from catching fire when the paraffin lamp, which his father had left alight early one Saturday morning before going to feed the cart horses. The lamp was under the linen, which was strung across kitchen ceiling, and had caught fire. His mother was in bed, as it was very early, and when woken she had to use buckets of water to put the fire out.

They had fun using the sand hole as a speedway track on their cycles.

He has many memories of the war years in Beighton: He remembers that the large field between the Dutch barn and the railway line was covered in cars, which had been commandeered from individuals, disabled, and parked in the field to prevent German gliders landing. He remembers a bomb dropping on the further side of the railway, missing the line by very few feet and that hole remains alongside the railway line to this day. If it had fallen on line it would surely have derailed the next train causing injuries.

On a nearby field he went with friends to look for shrapnel after a bomb had dropped, but was told by Mr Burton, the air raid officer to leave the field, and at 3.30 that afternoon a time bomb went off in that field. He remembers one night seeing thousands of chandeliers, lights of parachutes, coming down from German bombers; it lit up the whole village. He remembers two Mustang American planes crashing in Beighton near Cantley Corner: they hit each other. A 21 year old died and the other bailed out near the barbed wire road.

On the farm he remembers leading the horse which had an implement to hoe sugar beet, and the farmer steering from behind. The farmer said he could sit on the horse if he wished but when he did this he could not get the horse to walk straight.

BETTY GATHERGOOD, nee JAMES WRITES

I was born at Stone Corner, Beighton. The cottage we lived in hadn't any electric or gas so we had to have oil lamps and coal fires, and water came from a well. We had a radio that ran on an accumulator, which I had to go to Halvergate, to Mr Rowland, to take one to be exchanged and bring one back to get the radio to work.

Outside our house was a big stone that soldiers used as a mounting stone to get on their horses. An ancient battle was said to have been fought on a big field on the way between Beighton and Acle.

Rev. Walker, who lived in the nearby Beighton Rectory had a son who used to visit him by flying a light aircraft and landing on the same field where the battle had taken place, and then walked into the village to see his parents.

My mum used to scrub that stone every Monday, after she had finished the washing, to keep it clean; we used to sit on it and watch people go by.

MANOR HOUSE FARM

Manor House Farm. Photograph supplied by Dorothy Borrett.

This property is located at about TG382082.
    This farmhouse is a grade II listed building of red brick and pantile roof and was probably built in the eighteenth century.
    Buildings were marked here on the Enclosure map of circa 1803 and were shown as owned by James Littlewood.
    On the later Tithe map, area 74 was listed as "House & Buildings"; the occupier was James Slipper and the land owner given as the Rev Jeremiah Burroughs. The Rev Burroughs owned about 100 acres in Beighton according to the Tithe Apportionment.

    On the 1911 census the occupant was Henry Sanderson a fifty year old tenant farmer and the dwelling was listed as having eleven rooms.
    Mr Arthur Shearing was a later occupant followed by his son Arthur L. Shearing and more recently it was occupied by Paul and Valerie Mack.

Members of the Shearing Family in the garden at Manor House Farm, photograph supplied by Val Mack, nee Shearing. Bertha Shearing standing on left, seated Arthur and Bessie Shearing (nee Youngs), Brenda Shearing (nee Key) holding Valerie and Arthur L. Shearing holding Margaret Shearing, Fernley Paine (nee Shearing), and her children Katherine Paine and John Paine.

VALERIE MACK, NEE SHEARING WRITES.

Arthur Shearing and others were on Home Guard duty on the church tower when their cigarette ends caught fire to the thatched roof, and they ran up and down the tower with pails of water from the pond below to put the fire out ... successfully!

Herbert Futter, known as "Spot", who was married to Emma Langham, was the Post Master and a very colourful character. When a local landowner tried to shut off a footpath with a padlock, on the gate, Spot gathered a gang together to break the lock, and although PC Marsh was present, he did not stop the lock being broken, and the footpath was reopened.

When the well respected Rev. Walker passed by Spot, who was on a ladder, he remarked, "That's the nearest you'll ever get to heaven".

Rev Walker was also the victim of pranksters who relieved themselves from the top of the church tower, directly unto him, his remark was that, "I have just been urinated on!", and the pranksters said, "When you've got to go you've got to go".

Arthur L. Shearing moved with his parents, Arthur and Bessie and two sisters Bertha and Fernely, from a shop where pigs were slaughtered and meat sold in Chapel Road, to Manor House in 1919. Arthur was just three years old and can remember sitting beside his mother on a pony trap with his mother holding her most treasured possession, the mantle clock.

Bertha Shearing played the organ at Beighton Methodist Chapel for at least 60 years. She was very keen on music and taught Geoffrey Moll, Mary Langham and George Shearing to play the piano. Later in life an electric organ was bought so that she could carry on, without having to pump pedals. Her father, Arthur Shearing, was also a lay preacher. Bessie her mother, was very strict in not allowing work, or even cooking or recreation on a Sunday, so when cold ham etc was served for tea the grandchildren who visited had to keep their trip for a swim at Gorleston earlier that day, a secret. The Beighton Chapel had its' last service on 13th March 2005.

The Methodists sometimes used to have meetings on the pasture by Manor House.

At Stone Corner there is a large glacial boulder which was used as a mount for horses and has a pair of old cottages named after it. Ralph James lived there as a child and has memories of going to the shop for gun powder to light the oven! He recalls that Irish cattle coming from Cantley railway station being drove to the marshes would stop at the pond here for their first drink of their long journey.

Mr Milligan from East Runton used to stop at Stone Corner with his steam lorry to top up with water.

Sugar beet lorries used to pass by Stone Corner until 1966 when a new road was built through the pasture to straighten out the road.

Bertha Shearing

COXHILL FARM

This is located by the B1140 on Coxhill Road at about TG378095.
    No buildings were located here on the Enclosure map but buildings were shown on the Tithe Map at area 6. The owner was given as Henry Negus Burroughs and the occupant was Richard Read. Henry Negus Burroughs owned 114 acres in Beighton parish according to the Tithe Map. Richard Read was listed in 1851 living here as a farming bailiff.
    The farm was part of the Burlingham Hall Estate and was put up for auction on 1st August 1919. (NRO/MC389/65.729x9) It was Lot 5 and described as follows:-
"The compact agricultural holding situate in the parish of Beighton known as Coxhill Farm containing 119a 1r 24p with
Farm House and Premises and Cottage now let (with the exception of Ord No 49 let to Mr John Cooper Snr.) to Mr W. H. Cooper on a yearly Michaelmass tenancy at an apportioned rent of £180 4s 6d per annum.
The Farm House is well built of red brick with tiled roof and contains:- Hall, Two Sitting Rooms, four Bedrooms & box room, Kitchen, Pantry, paved and covered-in yard, with Dairy, Washroom, Cellar, Coalhouse &c.
The Homestead substantially built of brick and slate is conveniently arranged and comprises:- Cowhouse for 2 cows, Barn, Mixing House, Chaff Barn, Loose box, Range comprising Carthorse stable for five horses with gear, loose box, chaff place, and Three bay open cart lodge, riding stable with stall and loose box, Gig house adjoining, Seven bay open shed to two enclosed yards, four loose boxes and Turnip house, 2 enclosed yards with 8 bay open shed, 6 bay open shed, 2 bay open shed loose box and turnip shed.
Near the Homestead is a Brick and Thatched Cottage with Garden containing 2 living rooms, scullery, pantry, two bedrooms, detached outhouse and closet"

Some probable occupants include the following:
Robert Capon listed between 1868 and 1883. He farmed 160 acres according to the 1881 census.
Mrs Robert Capon, widow, was listed in 1883.
Albert G. Chapman was listed in 1890 & 1891as a farmer.
William Hayden Cooper listed in 1900 and 1919 as a farmer.
Walter Youngs in 1922 as a farmer, and again in 1925 and 1937 as a smallholder.
James Mallett in 1925 and 1937, listed as a smallholder.
Robert Youngs in 1925 and 1937 also as a smallholder.
Mrs Youngs was here in the 1940s.

Mr Ray Parker was a recent occupant here

GRANGE FARM

This farm house property was previously called **WALKERS FARM** and is located at about TG 383072 on Chapel Road. It was marked as Walkers Farm on the 1880s and 1950s OS maps but was called Grange Farm on the 1970s OS Maps.

Buildings were shown here on the Enclosure map, owned by James Amis.

On the Tithe Map the property is shown at areas 167a, 'Farm Buildings', and 168, 'House', as owned and occupied by Mary Walker., while the 1836 directory lists her husband Thomas Archer Walker as the farmer here. Buildings were shown here on the earlier Enclosure map owned by James Amis.

John Wright was a farmer here on Chapel Lane in 1911.

James Arthur Key was the occupant in the 1940s.

LINCOLN HALL

Located at TG39207, this was owned by St. Mary Magdalene College Oxford and was shown on the Enclose map. On the tithe map it was marked at areas 101 and 103 and occupied by William Stratford.

There was once an ancient 'hall' here but has long been gone.

In an old publication of Norfolk Archaeology on Miscellaneous Tracts Relating to the Antiquities of the County of Norfolk from 1891 we find an entry: *"The Rev E. Gillett exhibited a carved wooden helmet and crest, probably part of a monument: long preserved at Lincoln Hall, Beighton, formerly belonging to William de Waynflete; circa 1400"*.

(William Waynflete was the Bishop of Winchester and the founder of Magdelene College at Oxford.)

One of the remaining buildings here was converted into a pair of cottages for farm workers.

In recent years M. D. Wright and partners farmed the property.

Some recent occupants here from old documents include the following:

NAME	DATE LISTED	NOTES
Henry Rayner	1734	Farmer.
Jane Bellman	August 1776	Of Kings Lynn. Leased the property for 20 years @ £4-16s-6d /year. (NRO/MC929/1,800x3)
William Stratford *	1807 -1843	Age 80, farmer in 1841. Buried 9th March 1843 at Beighton.
Maria Wells	1841 - 1851	Age 70 in 1841. Sister of William Stratford.
George Maddison	1861	Age 28. Relieving Officer & Registrar.
William Howes	1881- 1891	Ag Lab.
Samuel Wright jnr	1885	Of Moulton, occupied the farm

NAME	DATE LISTED	NOTES
		land of Lincoln Hall Farm.
William Church	1891	Ag Lab.
Robert Tungate	1901	Age 39, groom & gardener.
Robert Church	1901	Age 37, Farm foreman.
Edward James Hylton	1911	
Arthur King	1911	Age 45Farm Steward / Bailiff.

* Reference NRO/BR276/1/0352 entitled 'Plan of Estate in Beighton and Moulton belonging to Mr William Stratford 1807' shows he occupied the property and house.

THE ORCHARDS

This property is located on Lingwood Lane and is a modern five bedroom property set in about 17 acres. In 1995 it was for sale at £185,000. In 2002 it sold for £425,000 and in 2004 for £545,000. In 2009 it was listed at £700,000.
 Mr David Pruton was an occupier in 2004.
 Ms Emma Taylor and Chris Dell were listed here running a business **East Anglia Alpaca Mill** making **Alpaca Fleece.**

OTHER LISTED OCCUPATIONS AT BEIGHTON

Most people till the mid to late twentieth century worked on the land as farmers and farm and agricultural workers. Several were in domestic service and some had occupations as outlined earlier. Some people were listed as retired, some as living on private means and a few people were seamen and fishermen. The following lists a few of the other occupations and people which were found in the old documents.

OCCUPATION	NAME	DATES LISTED
Tailor	William Barker	1836- 1858
	John Fowler	1877- 1883
Millner / Dressmaker	Martha Rowland	1858- 1864
	Elizabeth Loades	1871
	Louisa Nelson	1881
	Priscilla Myhill	1901
Boot / Shoe Maker	William Loads	1854- 1868
	John Bruce	1881
	Arthur Loads	1916
Carpenter	Charles Hall	1858 -1865
Carrier	John Myhill jnr.	1879
	William Homes	1883
Bricklayer	Samuel Wright	1871
	John Wright (& farmer)	1883- 1908
	Samual Hanton	1881
Builder	Herbert Chapman (& Undertaker)	1916- 1925

SYLVIA CRASKE, NEE WHITE REMEMBERS.

I was born at number 2 Council Houses on Chapel Rd Beighton in 1932. My mother had lived there since she was 17 years old. Dad, Percy White, came from Moulton St Mary. I lived here till I was eighteen years old when I got married.
    I started school in Beighton in 1937 and remember my first day. It was a wet day and mother put me in a yellow souwester. When I got to school I could not undo it and asked the teacher to help but I had to keep in on till after prayers were said. The school only had two rooms, and my first infant teacher was Maud Gilbert. The head at that time was Mrs Hargraves. Later Mrs Ruby Ling became the infant teacher and Mrs Lettall was the head teacher. I remember Mrs Ling used to write some times-tables on the blackboard, and on top she would put a halfpenny and an aniseed ball. These were an incentive for us to learn the tables and if you got them all right you got the prize, but this was rarely achieved. I remember that Mrs Lettall loved her poetry.
    The playground was at the front of the school and gardens at the rear. There was a circle in the centre of the garden, which was the teachers' area, and the four corner sections were for the children.
    After WWII was declared we were issued with gasmasks at Beighton School and were told that if the siren sounded we were to go through the back gate and assemble at the Rectory.
    On the 5 January 1942 I left the Beighton School and went to Lingwood school.
    The day war broke out I was outside riding an old rusty bike when mother came from the next door neighbours with tears in her eyes and said the two boys next door will have to go in the forces.
    There was several money raising events in the village during the war years: some I remember were Warships Week, War Weapons Week and Dig for Victory, which were social gatherings with dancing and games for the children.
    We had evacuees in the village and we had four boys from Dagenham staying with us at one time. One day these boys watched mother dig up some potatoes in the garden and some time later mother found them digging all over her garden. When she asked what was going on they said they were looking for potatoes and mother had to tell them that they are only there if they had been planted. They did not know anything about gardening! These boys were not here long, but after they left we had other evacuees staying with us.
    We had a large dugout, corrugated iron covered shelter in the garden during the war and inside we had bed, table, chairs and tilly lamp and two spades in case we might ever need to dig our way out! We went to bed every night fully clothed so that if the siren went we could get to the shelter quickly. The siren was at Acle. I remember one time when the hedgerow at the bottom of the garden was alight from an incendiary bomb which had fallen nearby.
    Some of the games we played were spinning tops, hopscotch and sevensies. We also collected acorns for feeding the pigs. In the evenings we

sometimes listened to the gramophone. When I was about 11 the girl guides were formed and we had fun camping at Beighton Sand-hole and tracking around the village. I remember one day when I was cleaning my shoes ready for the guides: it was eight minutes past five o'clock, when there was a very loud bang. It was a V2 rocket which had fallen near the railway line and made a large crater. The train was due at 5:15 and had a lucky escape. I had started at Lingwood School when this happened and at lunchtime I, and some other children, went to the crater to search for shrapnel. I got back to school late!

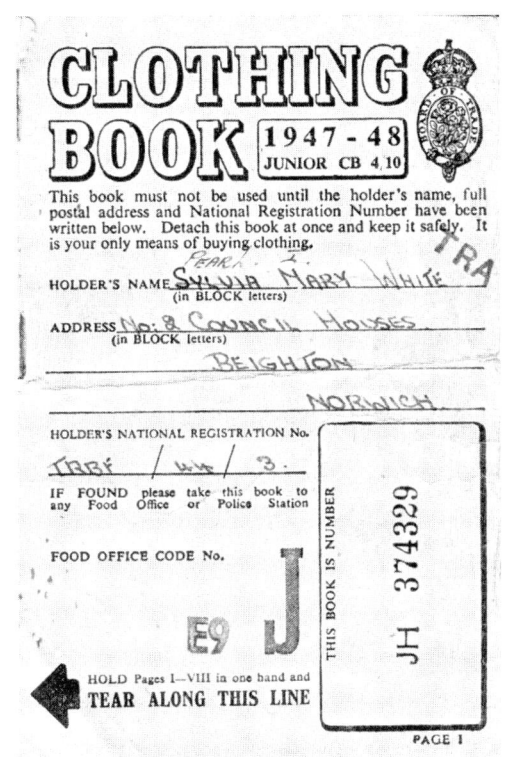

Our house had an outside toilet and when the bucket was emptied the contents were buried in the garden. My Saturday morning job was cutting up old newspaper for the toilet. There was one well to serve the eight houses. There was no electric.

I remember two shops in Beighton: Cators, and Futters, who also ran the post office. Everyone in the village had a slate and paid up at the end of the week. There was some deliverymen came round the village: Mathies the bakers, the Co-op from Acle, and Mr Gunns from Halvergate who sold everything from paraffin to groceries.

Dad worked, from leaving school till the day he retired, on the land for Mr Denny Wright at Morley House in Moulton. We often took dad his fourses : a corona bottle of cold tea and sandwiches. We had time off from school to help on the land during harvest time and I often led the Norfolk Punch horses taking the shocks to the stack.

I also went fruit picking at Lingwood where we had a 15 pound basket which paid 1s 3d when full.

Mother plucked and dressed chickens in the house to earn money. The house often stank of chicken inners and I had the job of taking the stinking inners out to the trench at the bottom of the garden. I, to this day, cannot eat chicken!

Mother also used to hang wallpaper for people to earn a few shillings. She also kept geese and rabbits.

I went to Chapel Sunday School and I remember Mr Cator at the shop always asked me to do a recitation whenever I went to the shop and then he'd give me a halfpenny. Mrs Bertha Shearing played the organ at the Chapel and she had a car and arrived at the chapel in her car. She always had to drive right around the village when she left the chapel because she could not reverse the car.

I remember Mr Waterson at the pub had a stallion and I often wondered as a child why so many people took horses to the pub! I also recall that Mrs Pitchers who was later at the pub was stone deaf.

PEARL CROSBY, NEE WHITE REMEMBERS.

I was born at 2 Chapel Road on December 6th 1935 the second child of Percy Dennis George White and Dorothy Marjorie White, nee Self.

When I was old enough to help mum with the housework every Saturday was 'turning out' day I remember. Same procedure every week! All the chairs from the living room were put into the hall; next job was to black lead the stove with either Zebro or a paste. All the door knobs were brass so they had to be polished. The fire rug was usually a 'piece mat' mum had made from old coats and trousers or anything else not anymore good to wear. They were heavy to shake. Windows cleaned and furniture to polish. A piece of newspaper was put on the table for the forks, knives and spoons to be

Sisters Pearl and Shirley Crosby at their 'Strawberry Tea' in their garden at Hopton Gardens on 21st June 1998. They raised £1,062 for charity on this occasion.
Photograph supplied by Pearl Crosby

cleaned. Another of my tasks was to scrub the outside toilet: that was a pail job then. Dad buried the waste in the garden.

No electric or running water. We had a paraffin lamp but we used candles for going to bed and having a read in bed. Washing was done with a bowl and tray on the living room table then we graduated to a little sink with a pail underneath to catch the water.

Mum had a wall oven for cooking in and an old copper for washing. Drinking water was drawn from the well. Mum used to iron with the box iron, you heated the block on the oil stove, that was followed by the flat iron. Mum was good outdoors and she was the one who built the goat's house.

Carn Close was once an orchard which went with the white house and a Mrs Farrow used to sell eating apples.

When Mr Norman Chalk owned the old rectory he had a lot of old carriages and opened the hut where he kept them to the public. You could have tea, coffee and cakes and he had a Victorian organ.

Percy White and Dorothy Self. They married on 26th December 1931. Photograph supplied by Pearl Crosby.

I remember a Mr Ward, who used to be a policeman, lived in a hut on a piece of land, belonging to Mr and Mrs Smith, near our house on Chapel Road.

MARGARET WARD NEE BURTON REMEMBERS.

I lived at Church Hill Beighton in a row of five houses which belonged to the Wright family at Moulton St Mary, with my parents and two brothers, Hylton, Nevil and one sister Beryl. Occupants of this row of houses were Mrs Olive Brown and daughter Fay, Mrs Norton and her family and lodger Mr Arthur Hall, then the Burtons, next a derelict property and finally Mr Coleman and his son and daughter, Percy and Maud. In the field opposite our front gate was an old railway wagon occupied by a reclusive gentleman a Mr Harry London, always known to us as "Old Harry".

My Parents were the last tenants to leave the house after it was considered uninhabitable in 1976 and moved to a council bungalow on Beighton High Road. The properties were then left in a derelict condition for several years until they were sold and rebuilt in their present form as a single property.

William Burton with Mr Wright's motor car. Supplied by Margaret Ward.

My father, was William (Billy) Burton and mother Alice, nee Pearson who originated from Freethorpe, a daughter of Fred Pearson, a shoemaker. My father worked at Morley House, Moulton St. Mary, employed as chauffer to the Wright family in the early 1900s, exact dates unknown. He later was employed at Norwich Motor Company and at Easticks Yacht station at Acle until he retired. Father was a Methodist lay preacher on the Freethorpe circuit and preached at various chapels within the area.

My eldest brother Hylton on leaving school at fourteen was employed by Mr Arthur Shearing, of Beighton delivering milk. Nevil worked at the blacksmith shops at Freethorpe and Strumpshaw and Beryl was in service in Yarmouth, and the Elms at Acle for Mr Jimmy Wright. All three served in the forces during the war; the boys in the army, serving in Europe, Burma, Italy and Palestine. Beryl served her time in the WAAF at the RAF hospital in Ely.

Nevil and Beryl Burton. Supplied by Margaret Ward, nee Burton

At Church Hill we initially had no running water supply or mains electricity until approximately 1955/6. Water was taken from a well in the front garden which supplied the four houses in the group. Rainwater was used for washing and laundry etc from water collected in water buts.
Groceries were delivered by Eddie Harris of Freethorpe and meat from butcher Frank Sutton at Acle, by Bill Staff. Bread was delivered by Sewells of Acle two to three times per week by a Mr Jones.
Father kept bees and two pigs in the back garden and mother had chickens, ducks and geese etc and their food was supplied by Frank Moll of Freethorpe. She made all her own preserves, pickles, jams and marmalade etc and was an extremely good and adventurous cook, who would not buy anything if she could make it.

The three eldest siblings of my family attended the village school in Beighton and were taught by Mrs Lucy Chapman and quite often spent part of the day standing in the corner with their hands on their heads for misbehaving in class, or so I have been told. Being eleven and a half years younger than my sister, I was the only one left at home during the war and spent a very happy childhood with my friends, Betty James from Stone Corner and Fay Brown from Church Hill. We all attended Beighton School. Some of my earliest memories were being taught by Mrs Gilbert from Moulton, in the infant room and later a Mrs Stokes. The head teachers were Mrs Lettall and later Miss Thirza Bond.

I left Beighton school aged eleven and then attended St. Louis Convent High School in Gt. Yarmouth. I left there at age fifteen and worked for the GPO as a telephonist at Acle exchange and then on to Norwich exchange. I met my husband, who was serving in the RAF at Neatishead and we were married in 1957 at Freethorpe Methodist Chapel. Then moved to his home town in Diss where we have lived since.

During the war I have memories of the German V2 rocket which landed in the field beside the railway line at Cox Hill in September 1944. We had a lucky escape with only a broken window from the blast. I was just going to Brownies at the village hall and remember leaving my mother a note to say don't let the dog in because of all the broken glass in the living room; she had been out at the time. I also remember her taking me to see the crater of a bomb which fell near Beighton White House and later finding out it was still in the hole and had not exploded. We certainly would not have gone so close if we had known that.

I attended Sunday School at Beighton Chapel where I later became a Sunday School teacher. I also played the organ at chapel when Miss Bertha Shearing, the regular organist was away.

I have memories of Sunday School Anniversaries when the Chapel was full to capacity, and the overflow of people was standing in the adjacent field.

Some of the Methodist Chapel Ministers were Rev George Jackson, Rev Howard and Rev Cecil Deeks, and Lay Preachers were William Burton, Sidney Grimson, William Beck Snr., William Beck Jnr., Frank Moll, Mr Sloper, Mr Pegg, Myrus Sutton and Alec Brock.

Our Doctor was Dr. Cyril Fletcher at the Acle surgery and Miss Cross was the dispenser.

The village policeman lived at Lingwood, PC Marsh, and then later PC Wright. Father was a Special Constable during the War.

The main transport was Caroline Coaches which ran a service to Gt. Yarmouth twice a week on Wednesday and Saturday.

BEIGHTON VILLAGE HALL.

The village Hall is located at about TG381078. Originally this building was the old parish hall near the rectory but it was moved to its present position in about 1949.

The playing field adjacent to the village hall was once used for football. This field was part of Beighton Manor House farm belonging to the Shearing family.

The Beighton Parish Council has its meetings here.

Old Time Dances were once held here, along with Over 18s Club and the Happy Circle. Table tennis and tabletop sales were held here.

Today the hall can be hired for children's parties and various group meetings.

Ladies Group at the village hall. Supplied by Peggy Francis.

PAM ADLAM, nee SPOONER RECALLS.

My Dad was Ernest Albert Spooner, one of ten children of Albert Howard Spooner and Ethel, nee Patterson. They lived for many years at Hantons Loke in Beighton. Albert and Ethel's family being so large some of the older boys slept in a shepherd's hut in the garden.

My great grandparents were William Howard Spooner (1852 - 1882) and Susannah, nee Gilbert (1852 1939). William, who was listed as a shopkeeper and as a shepherd, was an illegitimate child of James Howard and Maria Spooner.

James Howard was a married man listed as a shopkeeper and farmer during the 1830s through till the 1860s. He lived at Worlds End in a cottage on area 198 of the Tithe Map. Maria was a dairymaid who worked for James Howard. After James' wife Sarah died James and Maria eventually married in 1865.

Susannah Spooner at World's End. Photograph from Pam Adlam.

WORLDS END

This is located at aboutTG381069. On the enclosure map several buildings were marked here and all were shown as belonging to farmer Samuel Hewitt.

On the Tithe map the "house and property" on area 201 was shown as owned and occupied by Samuel Hewitt: this was the location of the old World's End Farm house. The adjacent "cottages" on area 198, now called "Wheels Cottage", and "Windy Ridge" were owned and occupied by farmer James Howard.

1917 Spooner family photograph supplied by Pam Adlam. From the left: Albert Howard, Violet, Ernest, Sidney, Ethel with baby Joyce.

Margaret Spooner and Joyce Atkins outside the shepherd's hut at Hanton's Loke. Supplied by Pam Adlam.

Following Samuel Hewitt's death at the age of 81 in 1845 the farm was occupied by his son in law James Carver who was listed here as a farmer and cattle dealer till 1854. Mr. John Hewitt, a descendent of Samuel, became the owner of the World's End Farm and he was listed here as a farmer in 1858 and in the voter's registers from 1861 through till 1907, but lived most of that time elsewhere, spending only a couple of years here in the early 1860s and a few year more in the 1880s. William Loades was a farmer at World's End between 1910 and 1915.

Two further cottages were marked at World's End on areas 202 and 204 of the Tithe map, and these were owned then by Cyrus Gillett and occupied at that time by Henry Marshall and William George.

RONNIE MYHILL REMEMBERS.

I was born at **Worlds End Farm** in 1935; my parents were William Myhill and Katie Myhill, nee Baldry. My father rented the farm from Mr Wright of Acle. Father had a dairy herd and the milk was put into 10 gallon milk churns and taken to Southwood Road and put on a platform and covered by a cloth to protect it from the sun awaiting collection by the Milk Marketing Board.

Photograph supplied by Ronnie Myhill.

The old farmhouse was built of redbrick with a thatched roof and part covered with tiles, and had a date stone with the inscription "I S 1772". In those days there was a pond in front of the farmhouse.

Above: William Myhill with milk churn and young Ronnie in a barrow. Below: Young Ronnie Myhill on pedal car at Worlds End Farm. Photos supplied by Ronnie Myhill.

We had no running water. The water came from a well and it took 72 turns of the handle to get a pail of water.

We had no electricity until about 1960. We used paraffin hurricane lamps and later tilly lamps for light. When we first had a telephone installed it was a shared line with another property near the church.

We had bread delivered by Mathies of Acle and mother went to Acle every Thursday to get meat from Sutton the butcher.

I went to Beighton School till I was 12 years old and then went to Acle School on my bicycle. I left school at the age of 15 and started to work for my father on the farm. Dad had two other men working for him.

During WWII father dug a big hole and put a large chicken house there and covered it over to be used as an air raid shelter. The house was surrounded by cornstacks and haystacks and it would have been dangerous if incendiary bombs had fallen nearby. Father was on fire watch during the war years.

Our neighbours in the adjacent World's End cottages were Billy Goodrum and Wesley Stone.

I attended the Beighton Methodist Chapel and went on the Anniversary outings which went to Lowestoft and then on to Yarmouth for tea.

When the old farmhouse was becoming unsafe and the roof was sagging a new bungalow was built nearby and father moved into the bungalow in 1962.

I moved away from Worlds End Farm but returned here about 13 years ago.

Katie Myhill with calf. Supplied by Ronnie Myhill.

Billy Myhill. Photograph supplied by Ronnie Myhill.

An early photograph of World's End Farmhouse.

JOHN ETHERIDGE REMEMBERS

I was born at Worlds End cottages in 1924. There were eight of us at the cottage and the toilet was at the bottom of the yard. We had a tin bath and had a bath once a week. We had an oil stove in the house, no electric and no running water. Later we moved to number 3 Council Houses on Chapel Road.
    My father was Ernest Albert Etheridge, nicknamed 'Noushe' and he was for a time a manager on Arthur Shearing's farm, but later went to work at the Cantley Sugar Factory. My mother, Jane, used to clean the Methodist Chapel. I went to the Beighton School till I was 14 years of age, and one day a week we went to Freethorpe School for carpentry lessons. The teacher was Lucy Chapman and the infant teacher Miss Gilbert. When I was about ten years old I used to get the cows in and milk them for Mr Myhill. At school the boys all wore short trousers: my sister used to bring me my long work trousers so I could change behind the hedge before starting work with the cows.

As a child we used to walk from the village to Beighton White House with mother and pass the time here collecting car numbers: there were very few cars in those days.

I remember Mr Cator had a shop which sold everything and Mr Futter ran the post office. The farmer Mr Arthur Key, of Grange Farm, used to bring the milk. The doctor was at Acle and in those days you had to pay.

When we moved to the Council houses the White family lived next door in number 2 and the Brown family lived in number 6.

Billy Boast had an apple tree and we boys used to pinch the apples. Mr Futter used to call out "Catch 'em Billy!" Basil Self also had apple trees and I once ate so many I was ill.

I remember 'Ham' London lived in a hut and Jack Ward lived in a wooden hut in Moulton. Mrs Betts and her son lived in a railway carriage. Mr Hollis in Drakes Loke was a fishmonger and Mrs Loades was the ice-cream lady.

As a boy I played a lot of football and when I went into the navy I played football for the navy team. I was on HMS Nelson and after being demobbed I went to sea on a herring drifter for a while.

I married Joyce Atkins at Beighton Church in 1952. Her father, Henry Atkins, was the licensee at the Lord Nelson pub at that time. This pub was also called the **Cold Blow** and was made of clay. When Waterson had the pub he kept a big Suffolk Punch horse stabled next to the pub. One day Dan Postle got the horse out and came into the pub and said to Waterson, "Where do you want it? Upstairs?"

Mr Tan had the Golden Anchor pub in Moulton, and whenever he was pulling the beer he used to hum so we all called it "humming Beer".

CANTLEY CORNER is located at TG376067.

There were three dwellings marked at Cantley Corner on the Tithe map. They were owned by William Read. William Read was a farmer and lived in the cottage on area 215, and the others, on area 212, were occupied by the families of John Hanton and James Scott. John Read took over from his father.

In 1881 Elizabeth Curtis was listed at Cantley Corner running a general shop and later according to the 1911 census Robert and Sarah Myhill ran a grocers shop here.

Today only one dwelling exists inside the old Beighton parish near this location and that is Holly House at about TG378067 on the Old Cantley Road. This is currently occupied by Keith and Tracey Douthwaite. The Tungate family were previous occupants.

HANTON'S LOKE

This is a short roadway which runs from Southwood Road at about TG39760720 to TG3803070727.

On the Tithe map, of the 1840s, there were cottages here on area 182 owned by Christmas Thirkettle of Lingwood and occupied by 'Wilson and other', along with more cottages on area 180 which was 'Parish land & Poor Houses' occupied by' R Smith , W Waters and others'. Buildings were also shown here on the earlier Enclosure map, circa 1803, owned by Richard Thirkettle and Robert Graver.

In the voters registers the properties here were referred to as being on **Buckenham Road**. In the 1901 census returns, however, the loke was referred to as **Spooner's Loke** and widow Susannah Spooner lived in one of the seven dwellings. In the 1911 census it was called **Hanton's Loke** and a Mr William Hanton lived in one of the dwellings here. In 1911 there were six families living in the loke but today there is only two modern properties: The Walnuts and Two Gables: all the old buildings having been demolished.

The remaining properties in the late twentieth century belonged to the Hanton family. Mrs Mary Hanton of Glebe Farm on Acle Road, Lingwood (the widow of David Hanton) was the owner in recent years.

Two Gables was sold in 2006 for £175,000, and again in 2013 for £310,000.

One of the derelict properties on Hanton's Loke, circa 2003.

Beighton & Moulton St Mary Remembered

10/3 6 Bn. NORFOLK H.G.
1944

MOULTON ST MARY

In the Domesday Book Moulton St Mary was given as 50 households, 4 villagers, 25 smallholders, 2 slaves, 25 freemen, 2 lord's plough teams, 6.5 men's plough teams, 51 acres of meadow, woodland of 15 pigs, and livestock of 2 cattle, 20 sheep and 18 pigs.

MOULTON ST MARY VICARAGE

The old vicarage is a redbrick building built in 1854 for £700. It is located at about TG399073. One hundred guineas was given by the Lady of the Manor, Lady Catherine Melville, towards the cost of the vicarage build.

Following the death of the Rev. Bellman the vicarage was sold as a dwelling.

Henry Sharman was the occupant listed in 1901 and 1903, John Keith Edwards in 1907 and 1910, Walter Brown in 1911 and 1912, and Annette Marion Jane Kinder in 1913 and 1916.

In the 1960s this became part of the Moulton **ARABIAN STUD FARM**, run by the Wright Family. In recent years a campsite has been established here in the grounds by the Wright family.

Moulton Clergymen

Surname	First names	Date	Position	Notes
Cleyton	Richard	1591	Rector	
Broadhurst	Rogerus	1603	Vicar	
Browne	John	1612	Rector	
Essex	Thomas	1658	Preacher	
Essex	Thomas	1662	Vicar	
Essex	Thomae	1668	Vicar	
Brooke	Gulielmus	1668	Vicar	
Brooke	William	1668	Vicar	
Reyner	Thomas	1672	Vicar	
Brooke	Gulielmi	1672	Vicar	
Essex	Thomas jun.	1675	Vicar	
Reyner	Thomae	1675	Vicar	
Essex	Thomas	1677	Vicar	
Barron	Robertus	1681	Vicar	
Essex	Thomae	1681	Vicar	
Wilson	Richardus	1685	Vicar	
Baron	Roberti	1685	Vicar	
Richardson	Johannes	1689	Rector	
Sallett	Johannes jun.	1861	Vicar	
Pitts	Joannes	1709	Curate	
Pitts	Joannes	1711	Vicar	

Surname	First names	Date	Position	Notes
Sallet	Joannis	1712	Vicar	
Pitts	Joannis	1723	Vicar	
Fawcett	Horatius	1723	Vicar	
Fawcett	Horatii	1726	Vicar	
Carter	Thomas	1726	Vicar	
Carter	Thomas	1737	Vicar	
Giddings	Roger	1737	Vicar	
Candler	Philip	1738	Vicar	
Turner	Francis	1739	Curate	
Smith	Thomas	1740	Curate	
Allison	William	1746	Curate	
Candler	Philip	1769	Vicar	
Hicks	James	1769	Vicar	
Goddard	Thomas	1784	Curate	
Hicks	James	1788	Vicar	
Anguish	George	1788	Vicar	
Burges	George	1813	Vicar	
Anguish	George	1813	Vicar	
Goddard	Erasmus	1813	Curate	
Gillam	Isaac	1817	Curate	
Burn	Hyam	1820	Curate	
Baker	Francis Plumer	1823	Curate	
James	J. B.	1840	Curate	
Messenger	John	1852	Curate	
Bellman	Augustus Frederick	1853		Died 1896
Nevill	Ralph William	1899		At Beighton
Walker	William Robert	1930s		At Beighton

MOULTON ST MARY CHURCH

The church, located at TG4023806668, became redundant in the 1960s and is now leased to the Redundant Churches Trust.

St Mary is a small 13th century church, comprising nave, chancel, south porch, and round tower. The south porch is from the 15th century.

There is a 13th century marble font, and 14th century mural paintings were discovered here in 1848. These wall paintings depict the Seven Works of Mercy.

In the chancel is a marble monument to Edward Anguish, who is represented with his wife and children in the attitude of prayer, and near it are a double piscina and a tombstone ornamented with a double cross.

In the nave is a stone coffin, which was for some time used as a watering trough.

The roof was replaced in 1842

Beighton & Moulton St Mary Remembered

Moulton St Mary Church: photograph from John Pegg.

TO
THE GLORY OF GOD
AND IN
GRATEFUL REMEMBRANCE OF THE
MEN OF MOULTON ST MARY
WHO FELL IN THE GREAT WAR
1914 – 1918
GEORGE ADAMS. NORFOLK REGT.
WILLIAM R. ECCLESTONE. NORFOLK REGT.
HARRY A. DU ROSE. NORFOLF YEO.
HERBERT J. DU ROSE. NORFOLK YEO.
LIEUT. BERTIE R.W. CHAPMAN. S. LANCS. REGT.
HORACE W. SHORTEN. R. FUSILIERS.

THEIR NAME LIVETH FOR EVERMORE.

ALSO IN MEMORY OF
JOHN L. CATOR
ERIC J. GOOSE
WHO FELL IN THE 1939 – 1945 WAR

Old postcard of Moulton St Mary Church.

Part of the wall paintings depicting the Seven Works of Mercy.

MOULTON ST MARY SCHOOL.

The school was built in the 1871/2 as a mixed school for 43 children aged up to 14. School teachers were in the village before that date, however, as shown in the table below.

The site was given by the Lady of the Manor and she paid half the cost of the building. The rest of the cost was raised by voluntary contributions.

The school was built in a plain functional style from Flemish bond brickwork (now painted) with a slate roof.

The school was scheduled for closure in 1954/5 but eventually closed in 1962. The document NRO/C/ED129/67 has an extract from the school management sub-committee dated 14 April 1962 stating *"The committee authorised the Chief Education Officer to commence negotiations for the closure of Moulton St Mary Voluntary School"*, and a letter from Mr Reading to Miss Lewis stating *"Will you please note that it has been decided to close Moulton St Mary Voluntary Controlled School as from the end of Autumn term 1962"*

In 1947 a local committee applied to the Education Committee to have a surplus hut for use as a Moulton St Mary Village Hall. Sadly the local committee was unable to find a site for such a hut and Mrs G. Mallett at the Vicarage, Moulton St Mary had to write to the Education Committee to withdraw the application. (NRO/C/ED129/67)

In 1959 the Acle Secondary Modern School was opened and children aged 11 and over attended the new Acle School.

The Moulton School has since been converted into a private dwelling.

Moulton schoolteachers from old documents

Name	Date listed	Notes
Emma Harrison	1851	Age 22. School mistress.
Charlotte Harris	1851	Age 40. School mistress.
Eliza Gilbert	1851	Age 30. School mistress.
Ursula Wright	1851	Age 26, School mistress.
Elizabeth Blackwood	1861 & 1864	School mistress, age 36 in 1861.
	1871	No school mistress listed in census!
Miss Rix	1877	School mistress
	1881	No school mistress listed in census!
Amelia Goodens	1883	School Mistress.
Miss Harriet Morgan	1888	School Mistress.
	1891	No school mistress listed in census!
Ann Louise Newland	1892	Schoolmistress age 36, married George Dobson in 1892.
Miss Charlotte Cantile	1896	Mistress.

Name	Date listed	Notes
Florence Bugg	1901 - 1916	Age 42 in 1911. School mistress.
Elsie Carter	1901	Age 16, school teacher.
Mrs Ruby Eliza Ling, nee Flint	1920s -1950s	School teacher age 22 in 1925 when she married. Also at Beighton.
Mrs Thaxton		
Mrs Riches	1950s	
Mrs Palmer	1950s	
Miss Powell	1950s	
Miss Starkings	1950s	

Some recent occupants of the Old School House include Mr V. Gordon and Mrs Caldwell.

Mr and Mrs Arthur and Ruby Ling with Ivy Brady and Sybil Smith in February 1967. Mrs Ling was a schoolteacher at Moulton St Mary School for many years. Photograph supplied by Daphne Carway nee Smith.

Moulton St Mary School photograph from 1928

Top Row: Mabel Barber, Mary Wymer, Mary Langham, Gladys Blake, Muriel Barber Sybil Smith, Ethel Bloom, Marjorie Barber, Annie King, Ivy Shorten. Second Row: Eric Goose, Norman Dye, Barney Brown, George Dye, Olive Dawson, Mollie Smith. Olive Blake, Billy Cator, Albert Dawson, Wilfred White, Sydney Goose. Third Row: Roy Hollis Godfrey Porter, Stella Porter, Elsie Wymer, Edna Barber, Kathleen Brown, Florrie Grimmer, Sheila Woor, Hilda Mayhew, Isabel Weavers, Dolly King, John Grimmer, Frank Allen, Billy Shorten. Front Row: P. Bloom, ? Barber, Benny Grimmer, Wally King, ? Barber, Norman Frosdick, Sydney Frosdick, unknown, Victor Blake, Jacob Barber.

Moulton St Mary School Nativity play, photographs from 1956.
Top Photograph: Michael Langham, Barry Hubbard, Margaret Allen, Michael Roe, Janet Roe, Rodney Brown, Pauline Cator, Daphne Smith, Violet Kemp, Pat Cator, Valerie Goose, Herbert Smith, Hazel Stimpson, Irene Goose, Margaret Langham, Bridget Locke, David Hollis. Front Row: Joyce Forder, Robert Smith, Maureen Smith, Peggy Smith, Mary Allen Keith Francis & Robin White.
Lower photograph: Violet Kemp, Valerie Goose, Hazel Stimpson, Bridget Locke, Janet Roe, Pauline Cator, Irene Goose, & Margaret Langham.

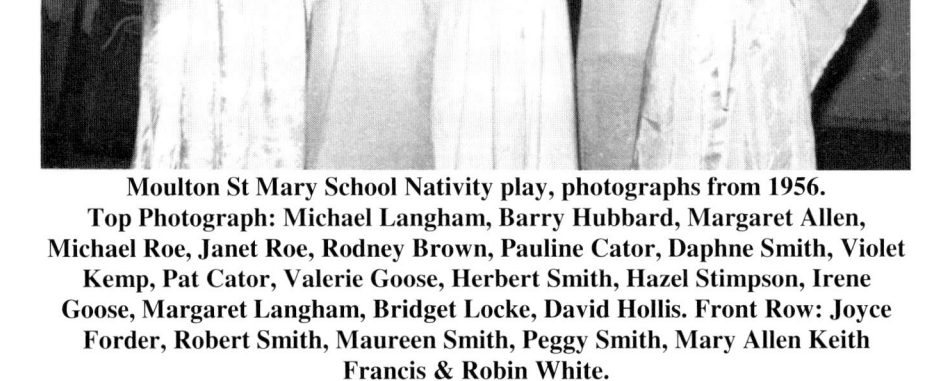

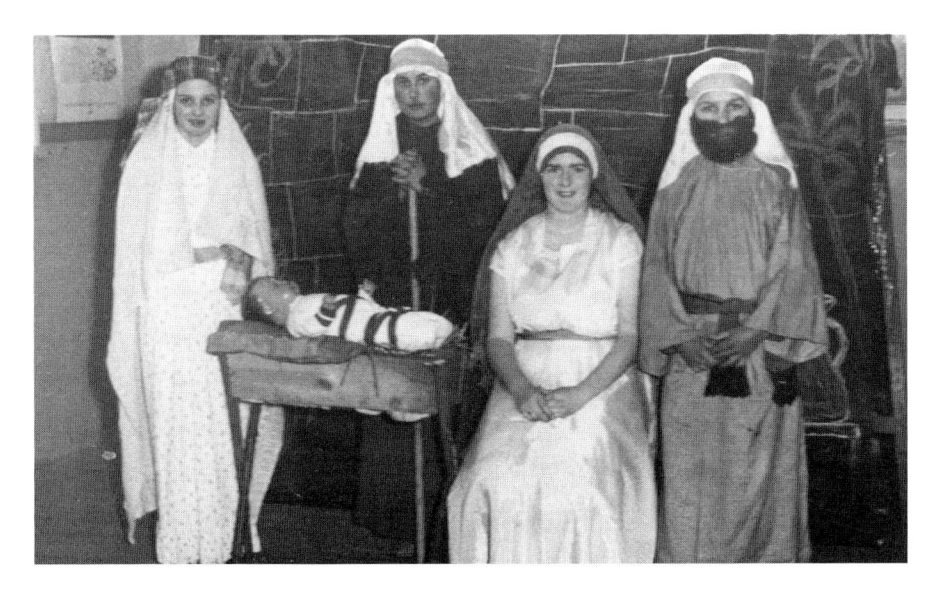

Moulton St Mary School Nativity Photographs from 1956.

Above: Daphne Smith, Joyce Forder, Pat Cator and Herbie Smith.

Left: Violet Kemp, Hazel Stimpson and Joyce Forder.

Photographs supplied by Herbie Smith.

Peggy Smith and Michael Carter in the 1956 school play 'Cinderella' at Moulton. Supplied by Peggy Francis, nee Smith.

1953 Coronation School Photograph: From the left: Robin White, Robert Smith, Daphne Smith and Val Goose. Supplied by Daphne Carway, nee Smith.

FARMERS AT MOULTON ST MARY

The following table names some of the farmers listed in old directories, poll books and census returns.

Name	Dates Listed	Notes
John Balls	1832	Tenant
Edward Rising Boult	1835 1880	300 acres in 1851 Church Farm (Manor House Farm). Tenant
Robert Howard	1835	Owner
William Boult	1832 1841	Age 35 in 1841, Tenant.
Samuel Howard	1836 1837	Tenant.
Elizabeth Porter	1841 1851	Age 77 in 1851, 10 acres.
John Walnes (or Warnes)	1836 1846	Age 30 in 1841. Tenant.

Name	Dates Listed	Notes
Adam Wright	1837 1866	Age 74 in 1861, 10acres. Cucumber Corner. Tenant.
Charles Gilbert snr.	1835 1841	Age 90 in 1841. Owner.
John Burcham	1841	Age 65.
Charles Gilbert	1841 1866	Age 64 in 1851, 20 acres.
Isaac Burcham	1849 1851	Age 4 in 1851, 83acres. Tenant.
John Broom(e) snr.	1841 1871	Age 44 in 1851, Balls Farm 200 acres. Tenant.
John Broom(e) jun	1869 1871	Age 35 in 1871 Woods Farm. Tenant.
Francis Allard	1859 1880	Age 41 in 1871, Morley House, 320 acres. Owner.
George James Woods	1858 1866	Age 30 in 1861, 82 acres. Tenant.
Robert Thirkettle	1832 1871	Age 66 in 1871, 14 acres. Owner.
Samuel Wright	1861	Age 42 in 1861, 14 acres
Samuel Wright snr.	1861 1891	Age 50 in 1871. (Was earlier a bricklayer).
Samuel Wright jnr.	1864 1912	Age 66 in 1911 at Morley House.
Thomas Cubitt Boult	1879	
Benjamin Porter	1861 1894	Age 44 in 1861, 28 acres.The Grove.
Robert Boult	1883 1888	Moulton Hall
James Thirkettle	1883 1885	Owner
Robert Thirkettle jnr.	1891 1901	Age 50 in 1891. Owner
Henry Wright	1901	Age 75, Cucumber Corner. Owner.
William R. Carter	1901 1904	Age 40 in 1901, Wood Farm.
James Wymer	1901 1908	Age 49 in 1901, The Grove.
Frederick Harvey	1894 1904	
Alfred Wright	1901 1911	Age 35 in 1911, Manor House.
Mrs R. Gillett	1904	Ash Tree Farm.
George Hubbard	1904 1937	Age 39 in 1911, Kennels Farm.
Mathew Hovells	1907 1912	Age 52 in 1911, Wood Farm.
William R. Thirkettle	1908 1933	
Denny Wright	1908 1937	Age 32 in 1911
Allen Kerridge	1911 1912	Age 46 in 1911, Grove House.
Edward William Burton	1916	Wood Farm.
James Arthur Key	1914 1916	Grove House Farm. Owner. Lived in Norwich.
Wallace Ernest Kittle	1929 1937	Wood Farm.
Benjamin Moore	1929 1937	Manor Hall.
Fred Sharman	1929 1937	Ashtree Farm.
Ernest Aaron Wright	1929	Grove House.
A Gladdon	1933 1937	Grove House

ASHTREE FARM

This is in Mouton St Mary located at about TG399067 on Ashtree Farm Road.
Buildings were shown here on Bryant's map but marked as **BALLS FARM**. This was called Balls Farm after the occupant at that time which was John Balls.
Buildings were also marked here on the earlier Enclosure map, and Faden's map. On the Enclosure map this was shown as owned by W. H. Ashurst, the trustee of Thomas Anquish.
It was listed still in the 1877 voters register as **BALLS FARM** but from about 1880 it was known as **ASHTREE FARM**.
On the Moulton Tithe Map the farm premises were show located on area 181 as 'House, premises & stockyard' owned by the Trustees of the Lord of the Manor, and occupied by Edward Rising Boult.
According to the 1911 census the house had 9 rooms.
The farmhouse is currently occupied by the Wright family

Some occupants from voter registers, census returns and directories include the following.

Occupant	Dates listed	Notes
John Balls	1832 & 1833	£50 occupier farmer.
Edward Rising Boult	1835 & 1846	£50 occupier farmer. (born 1806) In 1844 he occupied & farmed over 200 acres.
John Broom	1849 & 1871	£50 occupier. Age 44 in 1851 farming 200acres.
Thomas Cubitt Boult	1877 & 1882	£50 occupier, farmer.
Alfred Howes	1885 & 1887	Occupier of farmhouse.
William Wright	1888 & 1889	Occupier of farmhouse.
Samuel Wright sen.	1888	Farmer & landowner.
Henry Penrice Frederick	1893 & 1896	'Occupier', but living at Burgh Castle in 1896.
Mrs Harriet Sarah Gillett	1897 & 1908	Widow of Robert Gillett, age 81 in 1901.
Miss Harriet Sarah Gillett (daughter of above)	1911 & 1916	Lived at the house, age 68 in 1911. (private means)
Denny Wright	1912 & 1916	Farmed the property.
William Burton	1922	Farmed here & at Wood Farm.
Fred Sharman	1929 & 1937	Farmer.

JOHN PEGG REMEMBERS.

From an early age I spent much of my school holidays in Moulton St Mary staying with my grandparents in their council house on Ash Tree Road.

Council Houses on Ash Tree Road. From John Pegg.

My step granddad Arthur Gilbert used to work for the White Line Oil Co delivering paraffin to local villages from his base at Acle in an old Ford van which had a huge tank inside.

At that time I was only about seven or eight years old living on Mill Road, Halvergate, and being his round on a Monday he used to collect me and then I would spend the rest of the week with him and staying at my nanny's house at Moulton. He also delivered to Reedham, Freethorpe, Beighton, Wroxham and Horning.

One of the best things I can remember was when he gave me my own money bag just like the one he used to carry all the change in, and when only a half a gallon was required I used to collect the empty can then fill it up and take it to the customers door and they would give me the sixpence halfpenny which it cost in those days and put the money in my own bag feeling really pleased with myself.

After we had completed the days round we would return to Acle, fill the van up ready for the next day and then go over to Ivy's café (Singing Kettle) which was an old converted railway carriage and have a drink and a cream cake of my choice. On the way home we would call in at Sarah's village shop where my granddad would buy sweets to take home: wonderful memories.

Once back at my Nan's house one of my favourite past times was sitting up in her bedroom watching all the sugar beet lorries on their way to Cantley Sugar

Factory laden with beet, or on their return full of lime to be taken to the local farms.

During the next few years I would spend lots of time at their house and it was during those years my Nan told me a couple of ghost stories which I always found interesting.

The first was at a given date and time a horse and carriage could be seen and heard travelling along Freethorpe Road heading towards Ash Tree Farm. As far as I know to this day nobody has either seen or heard of the said Horse and Carriage.

The second story involved my Nan and her sister. It was during a really cold and frozen night when my Nan went outside to collect her washing off the line. Due to the heavy frost the washing was all stiff as boards. This she pointed out to her sister looking out of the bedroom window, or as she thought. My Nan pointed to the frozen washing and waved to her sister but with no response.

On returning indoors my Nan asked her sister why didn't you respond to me when I waved to you up the bedroom window, her sister replied that she hadn't been upstairs in fact she hadn't moved from the living room at all!

So whose face was it at the window as there wasn't anyone else in the house at that time? We will never know and neither did they! Oh dear!

MANOR HALL FARM

Recent photograph of Moulton Manor Hall Farmhouse.

The dwelling is located close to the church at about TG403066 and has been called by various names in early documents such as MOULTON HALL, CHURCH FARM, HALL FARM and MANOR FARM.

The buildings were marked on the Enclosure Map as owned by Thomas Anquish, and on the Tithe Map at area 50, as 'House, premises, moat and orchard', owned by Lord Godolphin Osborne and Norton Edmunds as trustees, and occupied by William Boult.

According to the 1911 census the building had 7 rooms.

Some occupants from early census returns and other documents include the following.

Name	Dates listed	Comments
William Boult	1832 - 1847	Farmer, age 35 in 1841. £50 occupier. In 1844 he occupied 223 acres.
Edward Rising Boult	1848 - 1880	Farming 300a, employing 9 in 1851. £50 occupier. Died in 1880, aged 74.
Louisa Eliza Boult	1881	Widow of Edward; farmer of 220a, employs 8 men & 2 boys
Samuel Wright	1891	Farmer, age 70. (Wife Sarah)
Alfred Wright	1900 - 1911	Farmer. Died 1911, age 36. Son of Sam & Mary Ann at Morley Hs.
Denny Wright	1912 - 1916	Farmed the property.
Benjamin Moore	1922 - 1937	Farmer
East Anglian Real Property Co. Ltd.	1940s	Farmers.
David Denny Wright		Farmer.

The ancient moat to the north of the farm buildings appears as only three sides, each about 1 metre deep. A slight dip in the ground level nearer the farmhouse is all that remains of the south side of the old moat.

The Wright family in the 1960s trough till the late 1980s ran an ARABIAN STUD from both here and at the Moulton Old Vicarage.

Manor Hall is currently occupied by the Innes family.

Recent conversion of some barns has taken place.

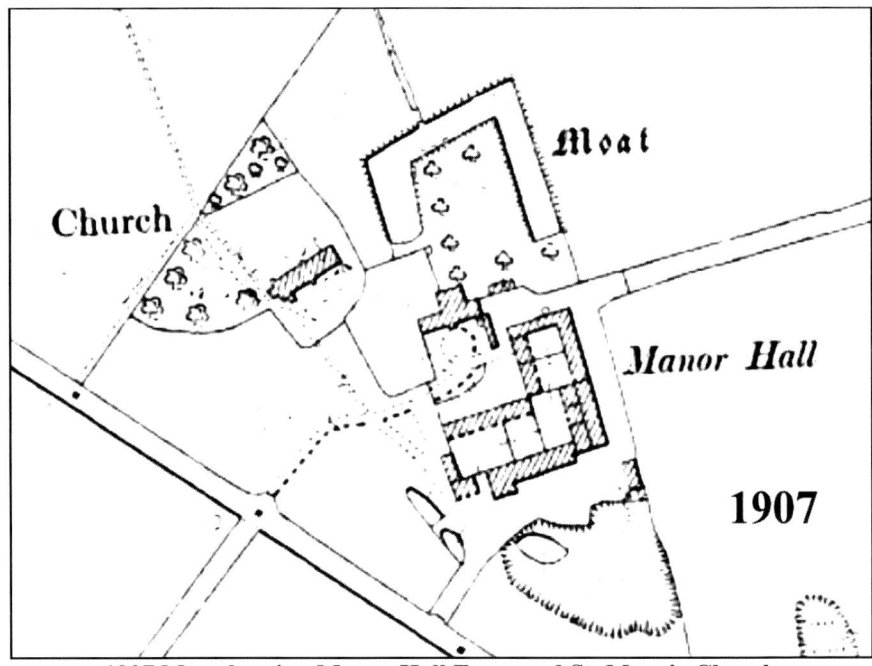

1907 Map showing Manor Hall Farm and St. Mary's Church.

Farmhouse at Manor Hall Farm in the nineteenth century.

HALL'S FARM

This is located at about TG404074, and was also known as the OLD HALL and HALL FARM.

At one time an old hall with a moat existed here just to the north of the existing buildings. Today at Hall's Farm there is cottages and the remains of the moat are still visible.

This was shown on the Enclosure map as the property of William Hall, hence the name Hall's Farm. William Hall owned 155 acres. On the Tithe Map the dwelling was indicated on area 24 as 'House, garden and premises', owned by Rev. John Hammond Fiske and occupied by Robert Howard. Robert Howard owned about 130 acres but occupied about 230 acres of the parish.

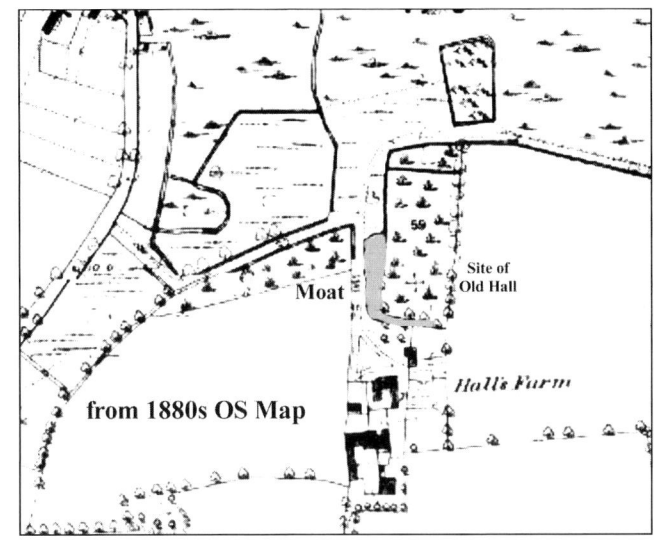

A later owner was Miss Fiske, listed in 1888, and Rev Frederic Ray Eaton was listed in 1902.

John Broom was listed as the occupier in 1851 as a farmer of 200 acres and again listed in 1853 and 1869.

The property eventually came into the ownership of the Wright family, and Denny Wright was listed as the farmer and landowner here in the 1912 and 1937 directories.

Hall's Farm continues to be associated with the Wright family.

A seventeenth century reed thatched threshing barn on the property is a grade II listed building.

Benjamin Wright, farm bailiff, lived at Hall's Farm Cottages for many years between 1885 and 1916. Photograph supplied by Corinne Miller.

MORLEY HOUSE.

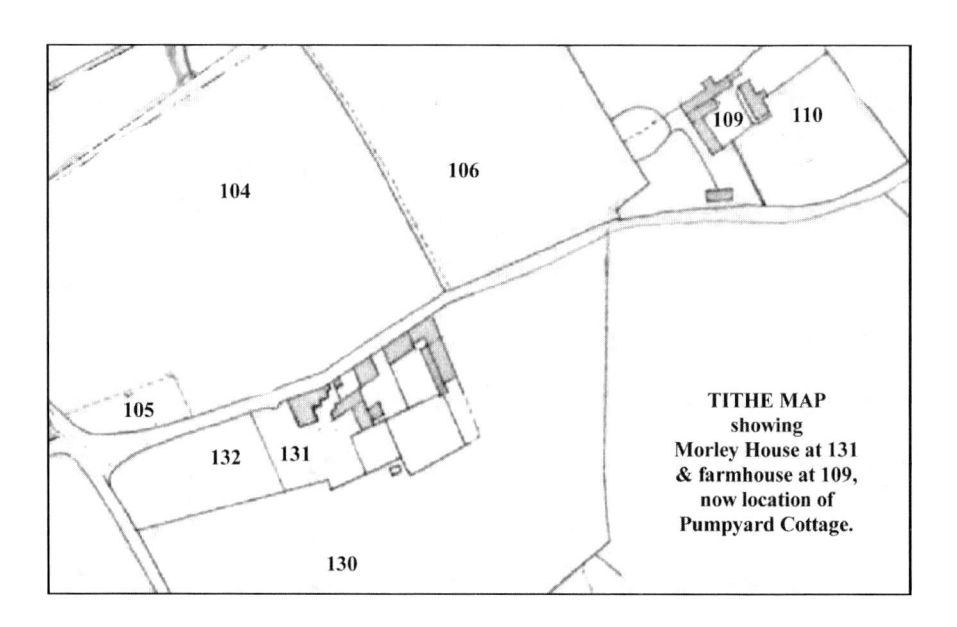

TITHE MAP showing Morley House at 131 & farmhouse at 109, now location of Pumpyard Cottage.

The farmhouse is located at about TG393076 on Morley Road.
Buildings were shown on the Enclosure Map and on area 131 of the Tithe Map as owned and occupied by Robert Howard.

Above: Morley House circa 1870s.
Below: A recent photograph of Morley House.

Francis Allard was the farmer here for many years. He was listed in the voting registers and directories at Moulton St Mary from 1860 through till about 1879 as a farmer and landowner. In the 1871 census returns he was aged 41 farming 320 acres employing 9 men and 6 boys. Francis Allard was also listed in the 1888 directory living at Trimingham but was still named as a major land owner in Moulton St Mary.

Samuel Wright was the farmer occupant here for many years: he was listed here in the 1901 census aged 56, and was here till he died in 1917.

According to the 1911 census returns the house had nine rooms.

Later, his son Denny Wright was the farmer here. The property has continued to be occupied by the descendents of the Wright family.

Over the last two decades some of the barns associated with the farm have been converted and sold as private dwellings.

Wright's long serving farm workers: Organ King, Percy White, Jack Burton, William Smith, Sam Bloom, and Mr Allen. Photograph supplied by Peggy Francis, nee Smith.

Long serving workers receiving their Awards at the Royal Norfolk Show.

WOOD FARM

This was located at about TG399083, on the roadway now called Kittles Road. The buildings were shown on the Enclosure Map of circa 1801, and on the Tithe Map at area 170 as 'house and premises' belonging to the trustees of the Lord of the Manor and occupied by John Broom(e).

The 1911 census records that the property had 8 rooms.

All of the buildings were demolished before 1980 but the farmland continues in the hands of the descendants of Samuel Wright's family.

Some occupants of the farmhouse include the following:

Name	Dates Listed	Notes
John Broom Snr.	1830s 1840s	Farmer.
George James Woods	1855 1865	Age 30 in 1861, Farming 82acres, employing 1 man & 1 boy.
John Broom Jnr.	1865 1875	Age 35 in 1871, farmer.
Thomas Youngs	1885 1894	Age 61 in 1891, Ag Lab.
William Reeve	1897 1900	Farmer.
William R. Carter	1901 1904	Age 40 in 1901, farmer.
Mathew Hovells	1907 1914	Age 52 in 1911, farmer.
Edward William Burton	1916 1922	Also farmed at Ashtree Farm.
Wallace Ernest Kittle	1929 1937	Farmer.
Lenny Rose	1940s	
Samuel Wright		Farmer.

FRED ROSE RECALLS

I was born on 22nd May 1944 at Wood Farm Moulton St Mary, Norfolk

On the morning I was born the midwife asked my father for a bowl of water; we did not have running water then but a large water butt outside. Well, being late May, the water was quite low in the Butt, and father had to reach low inside. At the same time there was a big explosion near by and my oldest brother told me father was white with the echo in the butt.

Another time when I was about 7 months old my uncle was home on sick leave; he had been in the desert and was shot through the side of his throat. At this time the local home guard decided to hold an exercise to see if they could form a road block across the road leading from Acle to Reedham, at a junction now known as Carters Car Corner. The object was to see if a soldier could get through the road block without being caught. Well my uncle being a trained sergeant in the desert campaign was well up on this type of game so he asked my mother to remove the base panel out of my big old pram so it left an open space big enough for him to get his bum in and his knees bent up near his chest. Mother covered him with some blankets and then they set off down the farm track and left at the bottom towards Moulton, when she arrived at the road block all the home guard blokes that were there knew my mother well and all they said was, "What's Lenny sent you out Violet! Lazy old bugger he is!"

When my mother got about a hundred yards passed the road block she stopped and my uncle got out of the pram in his army sergeants uniform and called back to them, then he walked back and they all had a good laugh about it.

My fathers name was Lenny Rose, originated from Wickhampton. During the war he was in the home guard and used to bike from Moulton to Reedham, to walk up and down the swing bridge with a broom stick on his shoulder, then he got permission to carry his own old twelve bore instead of the broom stick. His old pal was 'Widley' Carter, I think he was an uncle to the Carter family that now run the car lot; another friend of theirs was 'Puddy' Smith, that sometime after the war was out shooting and accidently shot himself.

SHOPKEEPERS AT MOULTON ST MARY.

No shops or shopkeepers were listed in the 1836, 1845, 1854 directories or in the 1861 census. No shops exist in the village today.

Shopkeepers Names	Dates listed	Notes
Charles Tills	1865 - 1869 & 1879	Beer house in 1864 Blacksmith & sub-postmaster in 1879.
Robert Tills	1869 1877	Age 76 in 1871 grocer. Earlier a blacksmith, son of Charles.
Emily Howes	1871	Age 27, grocer.
Thomas Howes	1871 1888	& Hawker, age 27 in 1871.
Adam W. Collins	1888 -1916	& Post office & boot & shoemaker, age 45 in 1891.
Mary A. Collins	1891	Age 38. Wife of Adam.
Marian Thurston	1891	Age 49, on Southwood Rd. Her husband Edward was fish hawker & dealer, age 49
George Ephraim Lorne	1929	Grocer & Post office.
Mrs Daisy Towler	1933 1937	Grocer & Post office.
Millicent Sarah Waters- Bloom	1937 1985	Shop & Post mistress.
Ivy Dye (nee Tooley)		

POST OFFICE AT MOULTON

No post master was listed in the early directories until the 1879 directory. The first Post Office was shown on the 1886 OS map near the junction with Morley Road near Peacocks Corner at the old blacksmith's shop.

The 1904 directory states: *"Post & Postal Order Office: Adam W. Collins, sub-postmaster. Letters from Norwich arrive at 6.30 am & 4.25 pm for callers only: dispatched at 6.25 am & 4.05 pm; there is no Sunday post. Acle is the nearest Money Order & Telegraph Office"*.

The post office moved, before the 1907 OS map was drawn, to a building close to the school on Acle Road. In 1937 the post office moved across the road when Sarah Bloom opened a shop almost opposite the previous post office.

Top: Moulton St Mary Post Office in the 1970s. Bottom: Millicent Sarah Waters-Bloom in the 1940s. Photos supplied by Violet Edwards, nee Kemp.

This last post office and shop was located at the property which was at the time of the Tithe map, of circa 1844, shown as area 120, 'House and Sheds', owned and occupied by Robert Thirkettle. Robert Thirkettle was in the 1851 census as a farmer age 45. The property later went to his son, another Robert Thirkettle, who was also listed as a farmer and was age 60 in the 1901 census. His son William Robert Thirkettle also became the owner and he was variously listed as a farmer, smallholder and market gardener. Following his death in 1933 the property was left to Millicent Sarah Waters-Bloom. Miss bloom in addition to opening the post office and shop here also kept pigs, chickens and calves.

The first telephones to appear in the village were in the mid 1920s. These were at Ashtree Farm, which was on the Freethorpe exchange, and at Morley House, which was on the Acle exchange. The Moulton Post Office had a telephone from the Acle Exchange sometime in the early 1930s.

DAPHNE CARWAY, nee SMITH, WRITES.

Pump yard Cottages. Supplied by Daphne Carway, nee Smith.

I was born at number 3 Pump yard Cottages on January 26th 1946. I had two older brothers Peter Smith, born 24th October 1934 and Malcolm, born December 19th 1937.

My parents were Sybil and Ezra Smith. Sybil was born at Appletree Cottage, Moulton St Mary. Her parents were Lucy (nee Banham) and Lewis Wymer.

My granddad Lewis Wymer worked for Denny Wright at Lincoln Hall farm looking after the cattle. My grandmother worked for Mrs Denny Wright at Morley House for many years. They lived at Blacksmith House on Morley Road.

My father Ezra and my brother Peter worked for Sam Wright at Wood Farm, Moulton St Mary and my brother Malcolm worked for Turner and Everson builders at Beighton.

Three Smith families once lived in Pumpyard Cottages: Bertie and Ellen Smith at No 1, Gladys and Jack Smith at No 2, and us at No 3. Jack at number two was my father's brother and he had three children: John, Maureen and Stanley. The cottages were owned by the Wright family and our rent was two shillings a week. The 3 cottages were eventually converted into a single dwelling.

Left: Lewis Wymer. Right: Lucy Wymer at the Blacksmith Cottage. Photographs supplied by Daphne Carway.

I went to Moulton St Mary School until about the age of 13 and then went to Acle High School when it opened in 1959. Mrs Ling was a school teacher at Moulton School and she lived in the village; we had three more teachers over the years: Mrs Riches, Miss Powell and Miss Starkings

I married Peter Carway from Beighton, whose parents kept the Old Nelson public house, which they ran as a post office and shop after the public house closed.

Appletree Cottage, photograph supplied by Daphne Carway. This property was shown on the Tithe Map of circa 1843 at area 67 as 2 cottages occupied by the families of James Wymer and Joseph Plummer, and owned by the trustees of the Lord of the Manor. It was sold in 1996 as a detached house for £97,500.

Mr C. Hubbard was the occupant at Appletree Cottage in 2001.

Mr and Mrs Thirkettle at No 2 Pumpyard Cottages in the 1920s.

Photograph supplied by Daphne Carway

PUMP YARD COTTAGE
This is located off Morley Road at about TG39460771.

At the time of the Tithe map, circa 1844, the property at this location, on area 109, was listed as "Farmhouse & premises", owned by Robert Howard and occupied by John Warnes. John Warnes was listed as a farmer in 1836 and was shown as a £50 occupier on 'Short Lane' in the 1847 voters register, indicating the short lane to the property from Morley Road was referred to as Short Lane. In the 1841 census he was listed as aged 30, and on the Tithe Apportionment he occupied 74 acres of land.

Many of the farm buildings on the tithe map had disappeared before the 1880s OS map was drawn.

Pump Yard Cottage.

The three pump yard cottages were converted into one dwelling with five bedrooms in about 1970. In 2007 the property with over an acre of land was put for sale at £477,000. The Conway family lived here in 2008.

ERIC WRIGHT RECALLS

My grandfather was Richard Wright born at Moulton St Mary in 1852, the seventh child of Samuel Wright and Sarah, nee Wymer. Like his father, Richard started as a bricklayer and builder but eventually became a farmer. At the age of 15 Richard joined the Methodists at Beighton where he eventually became a Society Steward and Class Leader.

HERBIE SMITH REMEMBERS

I was born in 1943, at 5 Hillside, Moulton St. Mary. These are my memories from the late forties onwards, and also of what I have been told.

Smith family photograph: William Smith with his wife Hilda and four of their oldest children; William, Bertie, George and Irene.

William Smith was my father and he worked for the Wright family, farmers and the main landowners in the area. For most of his working life he was the farm foreman. His work included looking after and breeding Suffolk Horses. These were bred at Morley Farm until the 1950s. Father was born in 1906 and died in 1994.

He began working for the Wrights in the mid twenties when he moved to 5 Hillside, Moulton St Mary from Scratby along with his mother who had been widowed before he was born.

He lived there with my mother Hilda and they brought up nine children born between the years 1929 and 1950. Mother died in 1981 and my father continued to live there until his death.

Beighton Football Team:
Beighton had a football team, Beighton United, which was certainly well established in the early fifties, and which may have been in existence before the war, continuing into the 1980's, and possibly beyond.

They were once in the Blofield and Flegg League, which later became the Great Yarmouth and District League.

Probably their biggest achievement was playing at Carrow Road in the Norfolk Primary Cup Final in the late 1959/60 season, in which they lost to Overstrand. The team consisted of Micheal Waller, in goal, Dougie Everson, Jimmy Hubbard, Donny Borrett, David Hanton, Jack Jermy, Des Mills, Irvin Hacon, Stanley Perfect, and brothers, David and Roger King.

Home matches at that time were played on a meadow on High Road situated in front of Shearing's farm houses. Cattle normally used the field, meaning that cow pats had to be removed before matches. There were no facilities and clothes and cycles were left under the hedges during the game.

In the late 1960s a new pitch was opened adjacent to the village hall, with the hall providing changing and toilet facilities.

Horses, etc:
The blacksmiths' shop at Moulton St. Mary was owned by the Wright family and was situated about half way along Morley Road by the roadside, not far from the cottages that stand back which were known as Pump Yard. It has now been converted into a bungalow.

Mr. Denny Wymer was blacksmith until approximately 1953 when Billy Smith moved from working on the land to shoeing horses and carrying out all the farm's repairs and harrow making, etc.

In those days Beighton and Moulton held a joint annual drawing match, now more commonly known as a ploughing match. This would be held in either Beighton or Moulton, depending on which field was available. People would come from other villages both to watch and compete with tractors and horses to draw the straightest furrow. Refreshments would be served from the nearest barn to the field where the match took place, and it was a very enjoyable day and always well attended.

Suffolk horses could always be seen working in the Wrights' fields until the sixties. Up until the late fifties they would show Suffolk horses at Ipswich and Peterborough and won many prizes.

At The Old Vicarage in Moulton there was an Arabian Stud Farm. This was run by Patricia and David Wright and they bred and showed Arab horses. The most famous of these was Ludo, a stallion, and Silver Blue.

My brother George, born in 1935, like our father worked with the horses and in 1969 he started as stud man with the Fairhaven family and moved to the Barton Stud. He was given a Racing Welfare Lifetime in Racing Award in 2009.

William Smith with some of the Wright family horses. The top photograph was taken at the Peterborough Agricultural Show on 2nd July 1929 with the Suffolk Mare 'Moulton Dazzle' which took first prize for Denny Wright at the show.

BeightonUnited Football Team circa 1959. From back left: David Hanton, Eric Myhill, Donny Borrett, Michael Waller, Stan Perfect, Des Mills, Charlie Smith. Front row: Godfrey Cator, Dougie Everson, Jack Jermey, Jimmy Hubbard, Roger King. Photograph supplied by Herbie Smith.

Builders in Beighton:
Turner and Everson were well known and respected builders in the area. They carried out all types of building works for local residents and farmers, and carried out the maintenance on Blofield and Flegg council houses.

The business began in 1946 and continued until the retirement of Cecil Turner and Douglas Everson at the end of 1980. The story goes that they were out celebrating being demobbed, and in a "merry" state lifted gates from fields of local farmers. They replaced them free of charge, but that was the beginning of their long running and successful business.

At first they ran the business from a wooden garage at Peacock Corner, Moulton St. Mary. This was owned by the late Mr Carter, grandfather of the present owner of the site, Gordon Carter. They soon re-located to High Road, Beighton, opposite the Village Hall on a site now occupied by new houses. There was a pair of now demolished cottages on the Chapel Road side of the site.

Following their retirement in December 1980 three of their long serving employees, Bruce Brister, Kenny King, and Herbert Smith, started Beighton Builders from the same site. When the site was required for building they needed to find new premises and in 1990 the business moved a short distance away to Norwich Road, South Burlingham. By this time Kenny King had retired, and the business continued until December 2002. The site is now the home of Beighton Building Services ran by Herbert Smith and his son Darren.

Moulton St. Mary and Beighton, other information:
Billy Langham was the roadman at Moulton, and could always be seen keeping the roadside ditches, known as "hols", clean, and sweeping the verges.

Mr. Langham lived in a cottage at Peacock Corner. He had a perfectly formed peacock within his hedge which he kept immaculately trimmed and from which the corner took its name. Sadly it no longer exists.

Billy Reid lodged at the Post Office and was a cobbler, repairing shoes for the local residents.

The roadman at Beighton was Mr. Goodrum.

Quarantine kennels were opened at Moulton St. Mary in the fifties and were owned by Mr. Hopkins. Later it was owned by Mr. Clarke and finally by Mr. Stretton. It was situated on a field behind what was the Anchor Public House not far from where the Garden Centre is now. Dogs and cats would be quarantined here for six months following their arrival from foreign countries. They were used by many famous people. The kennels closed in the 1990's when changes in regulations meant there was no longer a demand for it.

Tom Bailey kept the greenhouses at Moulton St. Mary which were later taken over by the Bringloe family. It is still run by a member of the family, although things have changed dramatically since the early days.

Beighton United Football Team mid 1970s. Supplied by Herbert Smith.
Back Row: Freddie Norton, Stephen Rowe, Trevor Webb, Peter Mayes, Jim Hall, Bob Brown, Dave Brown, Ken Adey, Tony Bland, Richard High. Front Row: Glenn Barber, Mervyn Borrett, Jack Norton, Mick Patterson, Paul Barber & Nigel Watson.†

Beighton Und. Football Club about 1950. Back row: Max Kiddell, Tom Etheridge, ernie Etheridge, Neville Burton, ?, Godfrey Cator, Charlie Etheridge. Front row: ?, ?, Dick Yallop, Dougie Everson & Charlie Etheridge.

LUDO an Arabian Stallion from the Stud Farm run by Mr and Mrs D Wright. Ludo won the Winston Churchill Cup for Supreme Riding in the late 1960s and early 1970s. The Stud Farm finished in the 1980s

92

CANARY CARAVAN TRANSPORT

Canary Caravan Transport was run from the Conifers on Acle Road. It was a small friendly family business which specialised in the transportation of mobile homes, lodges, holiday homes and all types of caravans throughout the UK.

Violet Edwards and daughter Jayne Smith

Canary Caravan Transport was run by Richard (Dick) & Violet Edwards from 1977. Dick was very forward thinking and helped to design the vehicles and trailers specifically to transport caravans and mobile homes. Following his untimely death in 1993, at the age of 53, daughter Jayne joined the business and continued until the retirement of Violet due to ill health. The business closed on 31 December 2009. The distinctive livery of green vehicles with the yellow canaries was a common site throughout East Anglia and the UK. Canary Caravan Transport was recognised as one of the oldest established firms in the business and was regularly recommended because of the good reputation and professionalism of everyone involved.

Canary Caravan Transport
Conifers, Acle Road,
Moulton St. Mary,
Norwich, NR13 3AP.
☎ 01493 750093
Fax 01493 751880
Professional Service VAT No 353 2583 57
Mobile Homes and Caravans fully insured

GOLDEN ANCHOR

This was an alehouse located at about TG 39760763, sometimes called the Anchor House. No building was shown at this location on the Tithe map of circa 1844 marked as area 116, which was owned by Henry Sharman of Halvergate.

George Gravener was first listed in the 1849 voters register as having a 'freehold cottage on the Green', and in 1851 he was a pork butcher, age 40. It is probable that the beer-house was started at these same butcher's premises some time in the early 1850s. Morgans Brewery took over the pub in 1901.

After closure in 1964 the building became a private dwelling. Mrs Agnes Annie Stephenson lived here in the 1980s, and more recently it was occupied by Mr C. J. Clarke.

Licensee	Dates Listed	Notes
GEORGE GRAVENER Snr.	1854	Pub not named!
ELIZABETH GRAVENER	1858 - 1861	Wife of George.
CHARLES TILLS	1864	Beerhouse & shop keeper. Pub not named. Later is blacksmith
DANIEL THIRKETTLE	1864 - 1869	Publican & Shoemaker in 1864. Pub not named. In 1868 listed as Innkeeper..
ROBERT SKIPPEN	1872	A butcher in1871, age 26.
GEORGE GRAVENER jnr	20.10.1873	Beer retailer. Pub not named!
BENJAMIN BRADFORD	19.03.1888	Market Gardener in 1881
JAMES HIPKIN	19.01.1891	
WILLIAM EDGAR LINCOLN	09.11.1891	Innkeeper, age 73 in 1901.
LOUISA LANCASTER	07.11.1904	
FREDERICK WENTFORD	06.11.1905	
GEORGE SIDNEY FLINT	08.11.1909	Age 28 in 1911.
WILLIAM FROST	20.05.1926	
JAMES PYE SMITH	02.01.1928	
WILLIAM JARVIS	11.02.1929	
ROBERT FRANCIS	01.12.1930	
WALTER SOANES	12.01.1931	
ADELINE ETHEL MAY SOANES	27.06.1932	
ROBERT FRANCIS	28.11.1932	
ALFRED ERNEST HENRY LEE	01.10.1934	
HERBERT JOHN TANN	07.01.1935	Nicknamed 'Hummer'
LESLIE RAYMOND KING	28.05.1956	
FRANK EDGAR PIKE	21.01.1964	licence not renewed 30.08.1964

Madge and Ruby Flint at The Anchor pub circa 1911.
Ruby was born in 1902 and Madge in 1905.
Photograph supplied by Ramona Knights, nee Ling.

Beighton & Moulton St Mary Remembered

Each year the Anchor public house ran coach trips. These went as far afield as Clacton, Skegness and Felixstow. This photograph is believed to date from the early to mid 1950s.
Back Row: Billy Langham, Mr Tan, Bert Gislam, Denny Wymer, Ward, ?, Ward, Billy Wymer, ?, Tony Burton ?, Sam Bloom, ?, Archie Buckell, Godfrey Cator, Noman Dye, Jack Stimpson, Reggie Hanton, George Tann, Sidney Goose.
Front: Percy White, Jimmy James, Billy Burton, William Smith Sen, Bertie Smith, George Locke Jun, George Locke Sen, Jack Burton, Jack Abel, Billy Read, ?, Freddie Lake and the coach driver.

96

BLACKSMITHS AT MOULTON ST MARY

On the Tithe map of circa 1845 the Blacksmiths shop was located at area 100, near Peacocks Corner, at about TG396078, and was owned by Charles Gilbert and occupied by Robert Tills. This was not marked on the earlier Enclosure map.

Moulton St Mary Blacksmith's shop on Peacocks Corner, circa 1870. The building in the distance is Lincoln Hall.

On the 1880s OS map, however, the Smithy is marked on Morley Road near the location of the old farmhouse, where Pump Yard Cottage stands, at about TG394077.

Some blacksmiths and wheelwrights from old records include:

Name	Dates listed	Notes
John Tills	1836	
Robert Tills	1841 - 1866	Age 56 in 1851. Later a shopkeeper.
John Tills	1851	Age 17. Son of Robert.
John Hood	1851	Age 23.
Charles Tills	1869 - 1879	Age 30 in 1871. Son of Robert. & post office in 1879.

Name	Dates listed	Notes
Edward Wymer	1871	Age 15
Benjamin Bradford	1871	Age 21.
Robert Gilbert	1871 - 1896	Age 22 in 1871.
Robert Callaby	1901	Age 50.
Percy Callaby	1901	Age 19
Bertie Chapman	1901	Age 19, apprentice wheelwright.
Robert Ransome	1904 - 1916	Age 41 in 1911.
Dennis Wymer	1901 – 1950s	Blacksmith, age 21 in 1901.
William Smith	1950s	Also at Freethorpe Smithy.

LYNDHURST FARM

This farmhouse is located at about TG400060 on Southwood Road and was originally called **THE KENNELS**. It was shown as the Kennels on the 1957 map but as Lyndhurst Farm on the 1972 OS map.

The buildings were not marked on the Tithe map, area 206, but are on the 1880s OS map. This area was owned by William Hall at the time of the Enclosure, circa 1801.

Sisters Emma and Rosa Wright lived here in 1901: they were daughters of Samuel and Sarah Wright and were listed as 'living on own mean's.

George Hubbard was listed here in 1908 and through to the 1937 directory

GROVE HOUSE

This was also often referred to as **FOUNTAIN'S GROVE** in some old documents.

This farmhouse is located on Porters Road at about TG400060, adjacent to the parish boundaries of Southwood and Freethorpe. It was marked on the Enclosure map, owned by William Collins, and it was shown on the Tithe map, of circa 1844, as 'house and premises' at area 190 and occupied by Elizabeth Porter, and owned by the executors of William Collins.

Elizabeth Porter also occupied the adjacent areas 187 and 188 which were owned by Andrew Fountaine Esq. hence the name Fountains Grove.

Grove House with ¼ acre of land was put up for sale according to NRO/BR184/2535, which was undated, for £39,950 after it had been modernised and reroofed. At that time it had mains water and electricity laid on and a new septic tank. The property had a lounge, dining room, kitchen/breakfast room, conservatory, entrance hall, two bedrooms, bathroom, and a garage.

Some occupants of the property have included:
Elizabeth Porter, age 65, farmer, in 1841, then her son, Benjamin Porter who was listed here in 1871, 1892 and through to1894.
Arthur Youngs listed in 1894 and 1896.
James Wymer listed in 1900 & 1911.
Alan Kerridge in 1912 & 1914.
James Arthur Key was listed as the owner in 1914 and 1916.
Ernest Aaron Wright in 1929.
Mr A. Gladdon in 1933 & 1937.

The barns here were converted into a dwelling, known as **GROVE BARNS**. Mr Key was the owner in 2000, and then Mr George Zavros. Grove Barns was put up for sale in 2014 with an asking price of £595,000.

QUARENTINE KENNELS.

These were located near to the old Anchor pub and were shown on the 1970s OS maps. These were run at that time by Mr & Mrs Stretton. The business was started in the 1950s by Mr Hopkins and was later run by Mr Clarke and then Stretton.
Following its closure Mr G. W. Willimott converted the property into a plant nursery in the 1990s.

CUCUMBER CORNER

This lies at the boundary between Moulton St Mary and Beighton.
Adam Wright, a farmer, was the owner of the properties in Moulton St Mary on areas 152, a house, and 154, a cottage, according to the Tithe map. He occupied the house and John Wright lived in the cottage.
In the Beighton parish at Cucumber Corner, areas 171 and 172, were cottages owned by Robert Howard and were occupied by Samuel King and John Howes families at that time.
Descendants of Adam Wright's family continued to own and occupy some of the properties here for many years. Adam Wright was still here in 1861 age 74 listed as a farmer of 74 acres, his son Henry was listed as the owner of property here and later Henry Albert Wright was the owner.
Area 213 on the Moulton St Mary tithe map near Cucumber Corner at the Southwood Road was owned and occupied by William Futter. The property here at about TG 38540684 is known today as Boundary Cottage.
The 1901 and 1911 census returns had seven families listed living at Cucumber Corner. Today there is only one dwelling known as Paddock House at about TG38620694.

G R CARTERS MOTORS

This business is located at about TG396077 in Moulton St Mary
The business was started in about 1960 and has become a well established company with a large range of low-mileage quality cars at competitive prices sold by Gordon Carter and sons Andrew and Mark.

G R Carters Motors in the 1960s. Supplied by Gordon Carter,

Charles Frederick Carter.

GORDON CARTER RECALLS
My father and grandfather lived here and my grandfather, Charles Frederick Carter, bought my father, Charles "Chinky" Carter, a lorry in about 1930. They delivered coal round the local villages and in the war years father started in Halvergate after marrying my mother Eunice Banham.
    I started here after coming out of the forces in 1957 after marrying my wife Patricia, nee Smith, who also lived in the village. Her parents were Billy and Hilda Smith and they had 9 children. My wife Patricia worked very hard with me to build up the business and also bringing up our two sons Andrew and Mark, who are now running the G. R. Carter Motors.
    In the early years I was a one man band, but I must mention my mate Aubrey Tooley from Halvergate: there was

nothing he didn't know about cars: any problems we always solved the same night. Also my brother-in-law Billy Smith from Freethorpe blacksmith's shop was a brilliant mechanic. I must mention one of our valets Leslie Springhall from Halvergate who was exceptional at his job, and Desmond Sharman who worked with us for 16 years as gardener and driver who was very dedicated to his job.

A young Gordon Carter in about 1950.

Mark and Gordon Carter with Percy Nichols.

I remember the village in the 1960s had one shop run by Sarah Bloom, and Billy Read was her lodger. Billy used to mend shoes and one occasion after he mended someone's shoes he went to a pub in Acle wearing the shoes he had mended only to meet the owner of the shoes in the pub! Billy also grew cress and took it to McCarthys in Great Yarmouth. One day he went to London and rang Sarah Bloom telling her he was in London; Sarah, who had not travelled very far from the village asked him, "How long will you be; about ½ and hour?"

I remember Sid Flint, my father's uncle, lived opposite in a thatched cottage in the 1960s and he kept pigs.

MOULTON NURSERIES

This is located at about TG398076.

Thomas George Bailey was listed as a market gardener in the 1929 directory and occupied these premises. He was still the owner in the 1940s. Jack Bringloe bought the nurseries in about 1952. In the 1970s Michael Bringloe took over the business. He demolished the old greenhouses and built new ones and opened a garden centre. Today it is very popular with a large range of quality plants and now has a gift shop and a coffee shop with a good selection of meals.

SOME EARLIER MARKET GARDENERS AT MOULTON ST MARY

Name	Date listed	Name	Date listed
George Warnes	1877 1888	Benjamin Bradford	1877 1888
John Lake	1883	John Hindes	1896
Benjamin Lake	1896	Fred Harvey	1901
William Bloom	1901 1911	Arthur Hilton	1904
James Kirk	1908	Henry du Rose	1911 1912
Robert Coggle Elvin	1916		

DES SHARMAN RECALLS:

Mr Sidney Flint raised pigs and sold them at the Acle market. He also kept many chickens till the outbreak of fowl pest. John Woodcock, Sid's grandson helped with the pigs.

Mrs Madge Woodcock, nee Flint, played the organ at both Moulton and Beighton Churches.

Sarah Bloom had the shop and ran the post office, and behind the shop Billy Read repaired shoes.

Billy Smith was the foreman for Denny Wright of Morley House. He used to cycle to the farmhouse once a week to collect the money for the farm workers wages. At home he and his wife Hilda sorted out the wages and then delivered them to the workers. Each wage packet was delivered wrapped in newspaper rolled up and tied with cotton.

At the age of eighteen in 1944 I used to visit the Anchor pub where I met interesting characters like 'Scorcher' Bloom, 'Siddy' Goose, Organ King, Freddy Kemp, Jack Smith, Bob Dye, Teddy King and Billy Frosdick. The landlord at that time was Homer Tann. At the pub we played skittles, darts, dominoes and sometimes we had a sing-along.

MOULTON ST. MARY POST CORN WINDMILL

Located at about TG 39440628, a mill has probably stood here for many years but disappeared in the early twentieth century.

A windmill was shown on Faden's and Bryant's maps, of 1797 and 1823, at this approximate location. On the Enclosure map of circa 1801 the property was shown as belonging to W. H. Ashurst, the trustee of T. Anquish.

On the tithe map of circa 1844 the mill, and house, are shown at areas 200 and 202 and listed as owned by Lord Sidney Godolphin Osborne and Norton Edmunds in trust of George Anquish, and the occupier was John Broome.

The Moulton St. Mary post windmill had a black mill buck set on a roundhouse. One pair of double shuttered patent sails and one pair of common sails powered two pairs of stones and a six bladed fan was mounted on a tail-pole behind the mill.

Norfolk News - 3rd October 1863
TO BE LET with Immediate Possession A MESSUAGE, WINDMILL and 3a. 0r. 32p. of LAND at Moulton in Norfolk, now in the occupation of John Youngs. For further particulars apply to Mr. Jas. Youngs of Wickhampton in Norfolk, Farmer.

Norfolk News - 10th September 1864
To be Let A MESSUAGE. WINDMILL and 3a. and 32p. of Land at Moulton in Norfolk, now in the occupation of John Youngs. For further particulars apply to Mr. R. H. Reeve, Solicitor, Lowestoft or to Mr. James Youngs of Wickhampton in Norfolk, Farmer.

Name of Miller	Dates listed	Comments / Notes
John Gravener	1816 - 1823	
Samuel King	1824 - 1826	
John Broom(e)	1830 - 1845	Miller age 34 in 1841. Farmer in 1851.
Thomas Napp	1841	Journeyman miller, Age 40 in 1841.
Charles Beck	1851 - 1856	Miller, age 31? In 1851.
? Mallett	1851	Apprentice, age 16 in 1851.
Robert Brooks	1853	
William Cozens	1858	
John Youngs	1858 - 1865	Age 27 in 1861, employs 1.
John Gaff	1869 - 1885	Age 33 in 1871. £12 occupier.
	1888	No miller listed!
John Disney	1890	
George Frederick Disney	1891 - 1899	Miller, age 34 in 1891.

FRIEND OF ALL NATIONS

An unusual item in a garden at Moulton St Mary, and located at about TG390073, is a large old boat.

The old boat that is at Moulton St Mary must be the oldest boat in Norfolk having been built by J. Critten at Yarmouth (presumably on Cobholm Island) as long ago as 1863. She was built as a private lifeboat for one of the Gorleston Beach Companies and was run by the Young Flies Company. Named '**Friend of All Nations**', she was 48 foot long by 21 foot wide and was powered by oars and sail.

Her history at Gorleston as a lifeboat is a bit of a mystery, but certainly in January 1866, she rescued four members of another Gorleston lifeboat, the Rescuer which sank at the harbour entrance. One of these unfortunately later died. The Rescuer was an unlucky lifeboat and when she sank, she was on her way to another vessel in distress in the Yarmouth Roads.

The 'Friend of All Nations' was often just called **FOAN** for short and certainly by 1925, she had been converted to a houseboat on the Norfolk Broads. She was hired out by Eastwick's boatyard at Acle and could be moved to different locations, sleeping up to eight persons in three cabins. In the 1930s she had a rebuild and was fitted with an engine. She remained part of Eastwick's fleet and was listed in Blake's catalogue throughout the 1930s.

During the 1950's, she laid at Thorpe St.Andrew and was later moored in a dyke at Wroxham during the latter part of last century. She was then purchased by Sandersons boatyard at Reedham. She later, however, sank and was in a bad way. Efforts to have her restored stalled and she was purchase eventually by a person at Moulton St Mary sadly as nothing much more than a playground attraction. She was taken to Moulton St Mary in 2011.

Friend of All Nation at Moulton on 8th August 2011. Peter Allard Collection.

EARLY HISTORY

The earliest evidence of human activity in Beighton and Moulton St Mary to appear in the archaeological record comes in the form of prehistoric flint tools. Only a few of these have been found, but have been identified as scrapers, flakes and borers.

A Bronze Age axe head has been found, and coins and pottery fragments have been found thought to be from the Iron Age.

Aerial photographs have shown crop-marks of ring ditches in the parish and these are possibly the sites of Bronze Age burial mounds.
Evidence of Roman occupation is from finds of pottery, coins and a brooch, while some of the stones in All Saints Church are believed to be re-used Roman stone.

No medieval buildings remain in the parishes but the moats near Moulton Hall's Farm and Moulton Manor Hall are from this period.
Probably the oldest building to remain in the area is the barn at Hall's Farm

POSSIBLE ORIGIN OF PLACE NAMES

Beighton: Begetuna is from Old English Beaga + tun meaning Beaga's farm or enclosure.

Moulton: Modetuna is from Old English Moda + tun meaning Moda's farm or enclosure.

POPULATION.

	BEIGHTON			**MOULTON ST MARY**		
Date	Male	Female	Total	Male	Female	Total
1801	98	110	208	87	83	170
1811	107	98	205	85	83	168
1821	129	115	244	95	90	185
1831	136	126	262	96	113	209
1841	147	141	288	110	125	235
1851	167	175	342	122	113	235
1861	185	180	365	132	127	259
1871	163	176	339	128	138	266
1881	128	144	272	111	129	240
1891	129	137	266	113	95	208
1901	106	112	218	110	100	210
1911	104	103	207	111	108	219
1921	136	125	261	107	110	217
1931	136	119	255	121	107	228
1951	240	228	468	Incorporated into Beighton after the Norfolk Review Order.		
1961	190	178	368			
1991			341			
2001			412			

NUMBER OF DWELLINGS

Census Year	**Beighton**	**Moulton St Mary**
	Total Dwellings	Total Dwellings
1831	51	28
1841	58	41
1851	68	49
1861	75	51
1871	72	57
1881	70	58
1891	67	59
1901	65	55
1911	59	56
1921	64	51
1931	67	57
1951	141	Incorporated into Beighton after the Norfolk Review Order.
1961	125	
2011	183	

OCCUPATIONS IN 1901

The following table lists the number of people with the occupations shown on the 1901 census returns for both parishes. The table clearly shows that the majority of the population worked on the land.

OCCUPATIONS LISTED IN 1901 CENSUS RETURNS	NUMBER OF PEOPLE MOULTON	BEIGHTON
Agricultural Lab.	6	25
Agricultural Engine Driver	1	-
Auctioneer	1	-
Blacksmith	3	-
Bricklayer	1	2
Bricklayer's Lab.	2	1
Builder & Farmer	-	1
Carpenter	2	-
Cattleman on farm	3	-
Clergyman	-	1
Coal Factor	1	-
Companion	-	1
Domestic Cook	-	2
Domestic Servant	3	5
Domestic Nurse	-	1
Dressmaker	-	2
Farmer	6	5
Farmer's Son (working on farm)	-	4
Farm Carter	-	1
Farm Labourer	10	-
Farm Servant	6	-
Farm Forman / Steward	1	2
Fisherman	3	-
Fish Hawker	1	-
General Gardener	2	4
General lab.	1	1
Groom	1	1
Horseman	1	5
Housemaid	2	-
Housekeeper	2	1
Inn keeper or Lic. Victualler	1	1
Lady's Help	-	1
Laundress	1	-

OCCUPATIONS LISTED IN 1901 CENSUS RETURNS	NUMBER OF PEOPLE	
	MOULTON	BEIGHTON
Market Gardener	2	-
Milkman on Farm	-	1
Mole Catcher	1	-
Mother's Nurse	1	-
Own Means	4	2
Parlour Maid	-	1
Pork Butcher	1	-
Postmaster	-	1
Rabbit / Vermin Catcher	-	1
Road Man / Labourer.	2	1
School Teacher	2	4
Shopkeeper (& Assistant)	-	2 (+ 1)
Shoemaker & Post office	1	-
Stockman on Farm	7	8
Teamster on Farm	6	7
Wheelwright Apprentice	2	-
Wheelwright & Smith	-	1
Workman	-	1

BEIGHTON SURNAMES FROM CENSUS RETURNS.

SURNAME	1841	1861	1871	1881	1891	1901
ABEL				2	7	
ADAMS	8	7	2	2	1	
ALLEN			1			
ANDREWS		1				
BARKER	13	14	9	14	10	6
BARNES		1				
BATLEY				1		
BAYES			1	4		
BECK		11	9	8	6	2
BELL				1		
BENNS	1					
BESSEY	1					
BEVERLEY		2	1	1		
BISHOP		1				
BLACKBURN			4			
BOATRIGHT?					2	
BREEZE					2	2
BRINDED	6	4			2	2

109

SURNAME	1841	1861	1871	1881	1891	1901
BRINDY?			3			
BROWN	6	1	4	4		9
BROWNE					5	
BROWNING			1			
BRUCE				3		
BRUNDALL	3	2	1	1		
BULLEY			7	7	5	4
BURROUGHS			2			
BUSH			1			
CAPON			2	2		
CARTER			3		2	1
CHAPMAN					1	
CURCH					4	5
CROMPTON						1
COOKE?						1
COOPER					1	3
CORY		1	1			
COWLES?				1		
CUBITT		2				
CURTIS		15	4	7		2
DANIEL						1
DINGLE		2				5
DREWETT						1
EBBAGE					5	7
ECCLESTONE		10	9	4	1	
ELLINGHAM		10	4			
EVERETT				1		
FARROW						2
FELLOWES		9		3	1	
FLINT				1		
FOWLER	10	7	11	4	2	
FOX			1	1		
FUTTER		9	14		6	
GATHERGOOD					1	
GARROD		1	4			
GEORGE		20	11	7	8	6
GILBERT		4	2	1	2	3
GOODRUM			8			5
GOOK						1
GOULTY				1		
GRIFFIN			1		4	6	4
GUNTON			9	14	3	4	6
HAMBLING					1	
HALL(S)			5	8	5	
HANTON	5	16	24	19	26	11

SURNAME	1841	1861	1871	1881	1891	1901
HARPER		1				
HARRIS		1				
HARRISON		1	1			5
HEWITT		5				
HOGGETT		2				
HOLLIS				1	5	5
HOODS	6	12				
HOWARD		2	1			
HOVELLS	9	6	12	14	11	5
HOWES	9	9	11	16	19	14
HUBBARD			6	5	9	
HUGGINS		5				
HUME					2	
IVES					4	
JONES	9	2	1	1	7	
KELLINGS?					1	
KING		1				
KIRK						1
KNIGHTS						1
LAKE		1	2	2	2	2
LANSDALL		4				
LAWN				4		
LING						1
LITTLEWOOD		3	2	1		
LOADS		4	1	1	1	
LORNE					3	3
LUBBOCK				4		
MADDISON		3				
MARSHALL	3	1				
ME3RRISON						1
MILES		1	1	1	1	
MILNE				1		
MINGAY	5	1	1			
MITCHELL				4		
MOORE						1
MYHILL		26	21	21	16	6
NEAVE		6	2	4	7	
NEVILL						3
NEWSON					1	
NICHOLS		2	2	2	5	
OAKLEY		9				
OLLEY				1		
PARKER		1				
PEACOCK		6	13	11		
PEARSON		1		11		

SURNAME	1841	1861	1871	1881	1891	1901
PIPE		1	1			
PETTITT					1	1
PLANE	5					
PORTER			1			6
RAIKES				1		
RAYNOR		4				
READ		10	5	5	2	6
ROBERSON		1	1	1	1	1
ROSE		2	9	4	1	3
ROUSE?			3			
ROWLAND		3				
SAUL	3					
SAUNDERS				6		
SCOTT		7			1	
SEAMAN		2	3			
SKIPPON	17	14	6	3	5	4
SMITH		8	4	1	5	6
SPINKS		1				
SPINNEY		1				
SPOONER		2	6	8	7	6
STANNARD			1			
STEVENS				2		
STEWARD					3	
STONE					1	
STOUT	1					
THAXTER						1
THIRKETTLE	2					
THOMPSON					1	2
TILLS		3			1	
TOOLEY					2	2
TRANSOM			1			
TRETT			5			
TUNGATE		2	1			2
TUNMORE						3
TURNER		4	10	1	1	7
TURTON?			1			
UTTING			1			
WARNES		3	1			
WATERS	3	1				
WATTS				4		1
WEBB					2	
WELTON?					Y??	
WILLGRESS	2					2
WILSON			10	7	1	
WITHAM				1	5	

SURNAME	1841	1861	1871	1881	1891	1901
WRIGHT			5	10	7	8
WYMER				6		
YEWELS		2				
YOUNGS		4	8	6	4	4

MOULTON SURNAMES FROM CENSUS RETURNS

SURNAME	1841	1861	1871	1881	1891	1901
ADAMS				1	2	1
AGUS	6	2				
ALLARD			7			
ANGUISH	6	4	9	7	4	4
ANNES		1				
ARCHER						1
BALLMAN					2	
BANTING			1			
BARBER						1
BARNES				1		
BARRETT			1			
BECK	6		2		1	
BELMAN		3	1	2		
BETTS	1					
BEWLEY		1				
BLACKWOOD		2				
BLOOM						3
BOAST					2	3
BOON			2			
BOULT	8	7	5	8		
BRADFORD	5	6	4	2	2	1
BROOKS				6		
BROOM	4	3	9			
BROWN			1	3		
BUGG						1
BULLEY						2
BUNN		2		2		
BURCHAM	3					
CALLABY?						9
CARTER						8

113

SURNAME	1841	1861	1871	1881	1891	1901
CHAPMAN	10	11	13	20	10	9
CHURCH				5	6	1
CLARK(E)		2				1
COLLINS					2	2
COOK				2	3	
COSSEY						1
CRANE			1			
CROFT					1	3
CROSS	1					
CROXEN						2
CURTIS	5		3	2	2	2
CUSHION					5	
DANIELS						4
DAWSON	4	4			1	
DENNY						4
DINGLE	7	12	12	6	5	
DISNEY					2	
DOBSON					2	
DYE		1				
ECCLESTON	2				2	6
EVERSON			1			
FANE		2		1		
FLOWER			1			
FORDER		2				
FOWLER		1				
FROSDICK					2	
FUTTER	4				2	2
GAFF			5	3		
GARE			1			
GILBERT	13	25	20	14	13	3
GILLETT						2
GOOSE			1	2	1	
GOTTERSON	1					
GOWN		2				
GRAVENOR		2	1	1		
GRIFFIN				3	3	4
GOODRUM						5
GYMER					2	
HALL		12	3			
HAMBLING				1		
HANTON						1

SURNAME	1841	1861	1871	1881	1891	1901
HARPER				1	1	1
HARRISON	7	6	3			
HARVEY					1	8
HEWITT						8
HIPKIN					2	
HOBBS						
HOGGETT			2	2	1	
HOOD		1				
HOOKER				1		
HOWARD		4	2			
HOWES	9	12	12	8	6	
HUBBARD						1
HUNN						1
JONES				1		
KING		16	16	6	10	5
KNIGHT					6	
LACK?		5				
LAKE				1	6	
LANE?			2			
LANGHAM					3	4
LEVER	1					
LINCOLN						2
LOADES			4	3	3	
LONDON						7
MALLETT	1					6
MARSH		1				
MEALE					2	
McLOUGHLIN						3
MILLER	1					
MOLL	5					
MORGAN				1		
MORSTEAD		1				
MORTIMER						1
MYHILL			1			
NAPP	1					
NEAVE			1	4		
NEWTON			1			
NICHOLS	4					
OSBORNE					1	
OLLEY						1
PARISH		2				

SURNAME	1841	1861	1871	1881	1891	1901
PLUMMER	6	6	3	2	2	2
PORTER	4	5	3	3	1	
POSTLE			3	8	1	
RAMM?				1		
RAVEN			3	3		
RAYNOR				1		
RICHARDSON					1	
RICHES	1	5			2	2
ROUSE					1	
ROWLAND			1	9		1
SALES				1		
SHARMAN						3
SHEARING	1		1	1		
SHORTEN	8	4	1	3	10	15
SHREEVE			1			
SKIPPEN			3	1		
SMITH	16		1	2	3	1
SOUTHGATE		1				
STOUT	9					
TAILOR		1	1			
TENNNT	1					
THACKER	4	7	6	6		
THIRKETTLE	6	5	12	13	9	6
THOMPSON	1					
THURSTON					4	
TILLS	9	2	9	10		
TURNER		1		4	2	2
UTTON	1					
WALKER	1					
WALPOLE				1	2	1
WARD						2
WARNES	3		3	4		
WATTS	8		1	1		
WILKINS		1				
WILSON			1			
WOODCOCK		1				
WOODS		3				
WRIGHT	9	26	20	16	20	22
WYMER	14	17	24	16	20	15
YOUNGS	15	19	20	14	10	3

REGISTERED VOTERS LISTED IN BEIGHTON IN 1915.

Abreviations used: Occ Occupier, Ow Owner, L&T Land & Tenement.

NAME	ABODE	QUALIIFICATION
Baker George	Beighton	Occ. House Chapel Rd.
Boast William	Beighton	Occ. House Buckenham Rd
Brinded William	Beighton	Occ. House Buckenham Rd
Brown Michael	Beighton	Occ. House Norwich Rd.
Bulley Alfred	Beighton	Occ. House Southwood Rd
Chapman Herbert B. W.	Beighton	Occ. House Near Church
Cooper William Hayden	Beighton	L&T Cox Hill Farm
Curtis Robert	Beighton	Ow L&T Cantley Corner.
Daniels Herbert	Woodbastwick	Occ L&T Near Cantley
Dingle Robert	Beighton	Occ. House Near Church
Everson Eli	Beighton	Occ. House Chapel Rd.
Ebbage Alice	Beighton	Occ House Buckenham Road
Fairweather Frederick W.	Beighton	Occ. House Near Church.
Frosdick George	Beighton	Occ. House Norwich Rd
Futter Robert Read	Beighton	Ow & Occ L&T World's End
Gedge Cyril William	Beighton	Occ. House Buckenham Rd.
Gedge John	Beighton	Occ. House Near Church
George George	Beighton	Occ. House Buckenham Rd.
George William	Beighton	Occ. House Near Church
Gilbert Henry	Beighton	Occ. House World's End
Gook Robert	Beighton	Occ. House Norwich Rd.
Grimson John	Beighton	Occ. House Chapel Rd.
Gunton William	Beighton	Occ. House Chapel Rd.
Hanton Ernest Henry	Beighton	Occ. House Southwood Rd.
Hanton Jonathan	Beighton	Occ. House Near Church
Hardesty Alfred Thomas	Beighton	Occ. House Near Church
Hollis Philip	Beighton	Occ. House Buckenham Rd.
Howes Thomas	Beighton	Occ. House Buckenham Rd.
Hubbard George	Moulton	Land Southwood Rd.
Hubbard John	Beighton	Occ. House Southwood Rd.
Hubbard Joseph	Beighton	Occ. House Chapel Rd.
Kerrison Roger	Ipswich	Ow Fee Farm Rent
Key Albert	Beighton	Occ L&T Chapel Rd.
King Arthur	Beighton	Occ. House Near Moulton
King James	Beighton	Occ. House Near Moulton
Lake Ephraim	Beighton	Occ. House Near Church

NAME	ABODE	QUALIIFICATION
Loades Arthur	Beighton	L&T Southwood Rd.
Loades William	Beighton	L&T World's End.
London George Edward	Beighton	Occ. House Chapel Rd.
London Timothy	Beighton	L&T Nelson Tavern
Myhill George	Beighton	Occ. House Chapel Rd
Myhill Jane	Beighton	Occ House Buckenham Rd.
Myhill John Henry	Beighton	Occ. House Chapel Rd.
Myhill Robert	Beighton	Occ. House Near Cantley
Nevill Ralph William	Beighton	Occ The Rectory
Pitchers George	Beighton	Occ. House Southwood Rd.
Roberson Ann Catherine	Beighton	Occ. House Norwich Rd.
Sanderson Henry	Beighton	L&T Near Church
Shearing Arthur	Beighton	Ow House Land Near Chapel
Smith William	Beighton	Occ. House Chapel Rd.
Spooner Albert	Beighton	Occ. House Southwood Rd.
Spooner Hubert	Beighton	Occ. House Southwood Rd.
Spooner Sidney Howard	Beighton	Occ. House World's End.
Thirkettle William	Norwich	Ow House&Land Sothwood Rd.
Tungate James	Beighton	Occ. House World's End
Walters Henry	Beighton	Occ. House World's End
Wright Albert	Beighton	Occ. House Southwood Rd.
Wright Frank	Beighton	Occ. House Chapel Rd.
Wright John	Beighton	Ow& Occ L&T Near Chapel
Wright Samual	Moulton	Occ L&T Church Farm
Wright Samuel Robert	Beighton	L&T Near Church
Wymer Dennis	Beighton	Occ. HouseNear Church.

Note: Buckenham Rd is now Hanton's Loke: Near Moulton is Lincoln Hall.

REGISTERED VOTERS LISTED IN MOULTON ST MARY IN 1914.

NAME	ABODE	QUALIFICATION
Bloom William	Moulton	Occ. House Acle Rd.
Chapman Robert sen.	Moulton	Occ. House Acle Rd
Chapman Robert jun.	Moulton	Occ. House Acle Rd
Collins Adam Wright	Moulton	Ow & Occ.House & Land Acle Rd.
Crowe Walter Thomas	Hassingham	Ow Land Acle Rd.
De Rose Henry	Moulton	Occ. House Acle Rd
Ecclestone Charles	Moulton	Occ. House Acle Rd
Flint George Sidney	Moulton	Occ. Golden Anchor
Gillett Harriet Sarah	Moulton	Occ. Ash Tree House

118

NAME	ABODE	QUALIFICATION
Goodrum Albert	Moulton	Occ. House Acle Rd
Grint Barney Harry	Moulton	Occ. House Acle Rd
Gunton William	Moulton	Occ. House Acle Rd.
Hall Edward Horace	London	Ow House Acle Rd.
Hanton Major Fairfax	Moulton	Occ. House Cucumber Corner
Hindes Samuel	Lingwood	Occ. House & Land Common
Hovels Mathew	Moulton	Occ. House Wood Farm
Howes Robert	Moulton	Occ. House Acle Rd
Howes William	Moulton	Occ. House Acle Rd.
Hubbard Emma	Moulton	Occ. House Common
Kerridge Allen	Moulton	Occ. House Fountain's Grove
Key James Arthur	Southwood	Ow House & Land Fountain's Grove
Kinder Annette M. Jane.	Moulton	Occ. The Vicarage
Langham William	Moulton	Occ. House Acle Rd
Langham William jun.	Moulton	Occ. House Acle Rd.
Ling James	Moulton	Occ. House Cucumber Corner
Mitchell Charles John	Moulton	Occ. House Acle Rd
Myhill William Henry	Moulton	Occ. House Acle Rd
Ransome Robert	Moulton	Occ. House Acle Rd
Read George Futter	Moulton	Occ. House Near Mill
Read Robert	Moulton	Ow House & Land Near the Run
Read Robert Futter	Moulton	Occ. House Near Mill
Riches Robert	Moulton	Occ. House Acle Rd
Shorten Benjamin	Moulton	Occ. House Near Mill
Shorten Horace William	Moulton	Occ. House Hall's Farm
Shorten Robert	Moulton	Occ. House Acle Rd
Thirkettle Elizabeth	Moulton	Occ. House Acle Rd.
Thirkettle William R.	Moulton	Occ. House Acle Rd
Turner Frederick Robert	Moulton	Occ. House Acle Rd
Walpole George	Moulton	Occ. House Acle Rd
Wright Benjamin	Moulton	Occ. House Hall's Farm
Wright Benstead	Moulton	Occ. House Acle Rd
Wright Denny	Moulton	Ow & Occ.L&T Manor Hall Farm
Wright Henry	Moulton	Ow & Occ. House Cucumber Corner
Wright Albert Wright	Caister	Ow House& Land Cucumber Corner
Wright Samuel	Moulton	Occ. L&T Acle Rd
Wymer Henry	Moulton	Occ. House Acle Rd
Wymer Lambert	Moulton	Occ. House Acle Rd
Wymer Lewis	Moulton	Occ. House Acle Rd
Wymer Robert	Moulton	Occ. House Near Mill
Wymer Walter	Moulton	Occ. House Acle Rd

ROLL OF HONOUR FOR KING & COUNTRY
BEIGHTON & MOULTON ST MARY.

FIRST NAMES	SURNAMES	NOTES
WALTER	WYMER	2nd Battalion Coldstream Guards. dangerously wounded 1916.
HARRY	BLOWERS	Sergeant 8944, 14th Battalion, Coldstream Guards.
PERCY	BLOWERS	Private 13471, 1st Battalion, Coldstream Guards.
VALENTINE	DU ROSE	Gunner 11994, 1st Battalion, Grenadier Guards. Wound 1914-15.
HARRY ARTHUR	DU ROSE	Private 1434. KORR Norfolk Yeomanry. Killed in action in Egypt on 7th December 1916.
HERBERT JAMES	DU ROSE	KORR Norfolk Yeomanry. Killed in action in France & Flanders on 31st August 1918.
JOHN H	CLEMENT	Sergeant 3132, 13th Hussars.
ALFRED JAMES	LING	1st Norfolk Regiment. Wounded 1917.
ELI	EVERSON	Acting Corporal 14626, Royal Field Artillery
ALBERT VICTOR	HANTON	Royal Field Artillery. Wounded in 1917
ROBERT FRANCIS	MYHILL	9th County of London. Wounded.
RICHARD HENRY RALPH.	NEVILL	Captain, 8th Norfolk Regiment.
FREDERICK	HOWES	4th Battalion Norfolk Regiment.
GEORGE EPHRAIM	LORNE	4th Battalion Norfolk Regiment.
BERTIE ROBERT WYAND	CHAPMAN	Second Lieutenant. 4th Battalion South Lancashire Regiment. Died of wounds on 13th June 1918.
GEORGE	ADAMS	Private 14427. 9th Battalion Norfolk Regiment. Killed in action in France & Flanders on

Beighton & Moulton St Mary Remembered

FIRST NAMES	SURNAMES	NOTES
		28th October 1915.
JOHN	FIELD	1st E Anglian Brigade Royal Field Artillery
WILLIAM D.	ROSE	Private 17284 3rd Norfolk Regiment. Killed in action in France & Flanders on 31st October 1918.
SAMUEL	EBBAGE	Lance Corporal 20766. 2nd Battalion Essex Regiment. Formerly 17491 10th Norfolk Regiment. Killed in action in France & Flanders on 3rd May 1917.
JAMES WALTER	KING	Army Service Corps
EDWARD	HUBBARD	Army Service Corps.
GEORGE ALBERT	PATTERSON	10th Norfolk Regiment.
ROBERT WILLIAM	GOOK	Private 32485, Somerset Light Infantry formerly Private 18370, 10th Battalion, Norfolk Regiment.
DENNIS	WYMER	Army Service Corps.
JOHN BENJAMIN	WILSON	1st Battalion Life Guards.
WILLIAM	MYHILL	Private 15948. 1st/4th Battalion Lincolnshire Regiment. Killed in action in France & Flanders on 1st August 1917.
FRANK	WRIGHT	Royal Engineers
LAMBERT	HOWES	Army Service Corps. .
ALBERT EDWARD	WRIGHT	Royal Engineers.
GEORGE EDWARD	RANSOME	Royal Engineers.
ROBERT ALFRED	SHORTEN	4th Battalion Norfolk Regiment
CHARLES E	CLEMENT	3rd Suffolk Regiment. Wounded.
LANCELOT	CROFT	Sergeant 14987, Machine Gun Corps. Wounded 1917
LEWIS ETHELBERT	MYHILL	Private 703681. 103rd Battalion Canadian Infantry (Central Ontario Regiment) Killed in action 15th September 1916.
ROBERT RICHARD	SMITH	Royal Navy. HMS Klondyke.
WILLIAM DAVID	SMITH	Royal Navy. Discharged 1915.
JAMES	SMITH	Royal Navy HMS Orotava.
CHARLES	HANTON	Royal Navy. HMS R Mackay.

FIRST NAMES	SURNAMES	NOTES
CECIL WILLIAM	HUBBARD	Royal Navy. HMMS Cheltenham.
ALFRED	GILBERT	Royal Navy. HMS R Mackay Discharged 1917.
WILLIAM	GOODRUM	Royal Navy Admiralty Mine Trawler.
JAMES	HUBBARD	Royal Navy. Admiralty Mine Trawler.
FREDERICK GEORGE	HUBBARD	Royal Navy. Admiralty Mine Trawler Died of pneumonia 1918.
HUBERT HOWARD	SPOONER	Royal Navy. HMS Attentive II. Invalided home 1915. Died 1917.
JOHN	BROWN, DSM	Royal Navy. HMS Attentiv
CHARLES	ECCLESTONE	Royal Navy HMD Active II.
FREDERICK	WYMER	Royal Navy HMS Euro.
CHARLES WILLIAM	HOLLIS	Royal Navy HMS Mischief.
REGINALD	CLEMENT	Royal Navy HMS Queen.
GEORGE ARTHUR	KING	Royal Navy HMS Repulse.
GEORGE	MYHILL	Royal Navy HM Mine Sweeper.
ROBERT	GUNTON	Royal Navy HMS Europa
CYRIL	GEDGE	Royal Navy HMS Serniramis
CECIL VICTOR	HOLLIS	Royal Navy HMT Maristo
FRANK	GRIMSON	Royal Navy HMD Moray Gem
JOHN WILLIAM	WEBB	Royal Navy HMS Achates.
JAMES	WEBB	Royal Navy HMS Sirius
JOHN WILLIAM	HANTON	Royal Engineers (Transport)
GEORGE ERNEST	FROSDICK	Private 5th Battalion, Norfolk Regiment. Severely wounded 1917.
WILLIAM ROBERT	ECCLESTONE	Private 4th Battalion Norfolk Regiment. Killed in action in France & Flanders on 13th August 1916.
FREDERICK CHARLES	WHITE	8th Royal Irish Rifles. Severely wounded. Discharged 1917
FREDERICK	BROWN	Private 26193. 8th Battalion Royal Fusiliers. Killed in action in France & Flanders on 4th August 1916.
HERBERT FUTTER	READ	5th Battalion Norfolk Regiment

FIRST NAMES	SURNAMES	NOTES
HORACE WILLIAM	SHORTEN	Private 76166. Posted to 2nd/4th Battalion London Regiment (Royal Fusiliers). Formerly 21264. 2nd Battalion Queen's Royal West Surrey Regiment. Killed in action in France & Flanders on 8th August 1918
ERNEST BERTIE	GEORGE	Private 24344, 8th Battalion, Northamptonshire Regiment. Prisoner of War 1918.
HARRY	LONDON	34th Royal Fusiliers. Wounded 1917.
WILLIAM	GODFREY	Corporal 124th Company Royal Army Ordnance Corps. Died on 17th November 1918 of pneumonia.
WILLIAM	LANGHAM	13th Royal Fusiliers. Wounded 1916.
GEORGE FUTTER	READ	10th Battalion Essex Regiment. Wounded 1917.
ROBERT FUTTER	READ	3rd Battalion Bedfordshire Regiment. Discharged.
ALBERT HOWARD	SPOONER	Royal Garrison Artillery.
MAJOR FAIRFAX	HANTON	Royal Field Artillery.
GEORGE	PITCHER	Royal Engineers (Water Transport)
CUTHBERT	FORDER	Private 13469, 4th Battalion, Coldstream Guards.
WILLIAM GEORGE	HOWES	Royal Engineers.
FRANK	ELVIN	14th Queen's Royal West Surrey Regiment
LEONARD JOHN	MYHILL	Royal Engineers
FREDERICK JAMES	ROSE	Royal Horse Artillery
HARRY	LING	1st Norfolk Regiment. Wounded 1918.
WILLIAM	RANSOME	Royal Marines
FRANK GERALD	WRIGHT	Middlesex Regiment. Wounded 1918.
BERNARD	BROWN	Royal Horse Artillery.
WILLIAM REGINALD	WEBB	Royal Warwickshire Regiment.

OTHER LOCAL BOOKS BY SHEILA HUTCHINSON.

Berney Arms: Past & Present
Berney Arms Remembered
The Halvergate Fleet: Past & Present
Reedham Remembered
Reedham Memories
Burgh Castle Remembered
Freethorpe Past and Present
Wickhampton Memories
The River Yare: Breydon & Beyond
The Lower Bure from Great Yarmouth to Upton
Halvergate & Tunstall Remembered
Cantley, Limpenhoe & Southwood Remembered